"The toughest part of leadership a
ing with people is often, simultan‹
part of one's work. Whenever and
potential for conflict. Dr. Houston Thompson has made a vital contribution to this aspect of leadership and ministry through his fine new book,
Conflict Management for Faith Leaders. His work is timely and both practical and theoretically sound. His various models of conflict management can
help anyone respond to moments of conflict in ways that can help preserve
relationships and promote unity. I highly recommend it!"

—Dr. John Bowling
President
Olivet Nazarene University

"Houston Thompson's years as a leader in the church and in the secular
and academic worlds bring a fresh perspective to how to lead people and
organizations in today's environment. His approach to the subject is well
thought through, with practical illustrations stemming from his own life
and work. Thompson shows us what to avoid and what to strive for in leadership positions. This work is a must read for anyone aspiring or already in
a position of leadership!"

—Dr. Jim Harriman
Director of Latin American Ministries, Francis Asbury Society
Director of Development/International Representative, Universidad Evangélica
Boliviana

"I wish I had read this book before starting my successful twenty-plus years
as a human resource professional and also serving as a board director for
not-for-profit organizations. *Conflict Management for Faith Leaders* offers a
new and refreshing approach to conflict management."

—John M. Keigher
Director of Systems and Human Resources
Midwest Transit Equipment, Inc.

"It seems almost every pastor/leader and every church/organization faces
conflict at some point. Dr. Thompson provides a helpful framework to
identify both the causes and resolutions to various levels of conflict—a
valuable resource!"

—Dr. Garry Pate
District Superintendent
Southwest Indiana District, Church of the Nazarene

"*Conflict Management for Faith Leaders* is an exciting and new way to look at the positive outcomes of managing conflict in your area of influence. Often as believers we shy away from conflict, but as Dr. Thompson shows us, there are various ways that you can manage conflict that benefit all involved. You no longer have to avoid it! Dr. Thompson explains how it can be used for the glory of God and for everyone's blessing. This book will help anyone involved in conflict resolution—directly or indirectly—to have a better understanding of how to manage it effectively."

—David Pickering
Director of Business and Human Resources
Olivet Nazarene University

"All leaders know that conflict management is an essential leadership skill. The best leaders know that conflict reveals opportunity for growth in individuals and communities, but only if the conflict is skillfully managed toward generative resolution. Houston Thompson has provided a field manual for 'faith leaders' that clearly and pragmatically guides the leader through the key steps of assessing, engaging, and navigating conflict toward resolution. This book may become like a wise mentor and friend to faith leaders."

—Dr. Jeren Rowell
District Superintendent
Kansas City District, Church of the Nazarene

"Conflict—no one wants it! However, it is a constant in the personal and spiritual life and wherever there are people together. Dr. Thompson presents useful handles to deal with conflict even when it is impossible to resolve it. I highly recommend his book to help us and organizations deal with the unavoidable."

—Dr. Christian Sarmiento
Regional Director
South America Church of the Nazarene

"For of all who lead others from a position of faith, *Conflict Management for Faith Leaders* is an essential guidebook. . . . the Six C's Model of conflict management provides the approach and underpinning to guide a faith leader in his journey."

—Dr. Jim Upchurch
Dean, School of Education (Former Public School Superintendent)
Olivet Nazarene University

CONFLICT MANAGEMENT
for FAITH LEADERS

Houston E. Thompson

BEACON HILL PRESS
OF KANSAS CITY

Beacon Hill Press of Kansas City
PO Box 419527
Kansas City, MO 64141
BeaconHillBooks.com

ISBN 978-0-8341-3244-3

Printed in the
United States of America

Cover Design: Matt McNary
Interior Design: Sharon Page

All Scripture quotations not otherwise designated are from the *Holy Bible, New International Version®* (NIV®). Copyright © 1973, 1978, 1984, 2011 by Biblica, Inc.™ Used by permission. All rights reserved worldwide.

Scriptures marked KJV are from the King James Version.

Library of Congress Cataloging-in-Publication Data
Thompson, Houson E., 1958-
  Conflict management for faith leaders / Houston E. Thompson.
    pages cm
  Includes bibliographical references.
  ISBN 978-0-8341-3244-3 (pbk.)
  1. Conflict management—Religious aspects—Christianity. 2. Christian
leadership. I. Title.
  BV4597.53.C58T455 2014
  253—dc23
                                                      2014009330

10 9 8 7 6 5 4 3 2 1

To my wife, Martha,
who journeys through life with me,
sharing in my calling,
believing in my vision,
supporting my dreams,
and loving me unconditionally

CONTENTS

ACKNOWLEDGMENTS

■ This book would not have been possible without the faithful encouragement of my wife, Martha. She supported the dream and sacrificed our time for me to complete this work.

The concept originated in a telephone conversation with Dr. Ed Thomas at Mount Vernon Nazarene University. Ed contacted me about writing a chapter for a textbook on this topic. The research took on a life of its own. The chapter was written, but the work continued to live.

I shared some of the research with doctoral learners in a class I facilitated. Dr. Bonnie Perry, director of Beacon Hill Press for Nazarene Publishing House, was in that class. She encouraged me to think about developing the material into a book. Her encouragement and guidance are much appreciated.

I want to thank Richard Buckner, ministry product line editor for Beacon Hill Press, for his thorough editing and guidance.

I want to thank colleagues and friends who prayed for me and encouraged me along the way.

I thank God, who has given me strength and energy not only to live but also to serve.

INTRODUCTION

■ Growing up as a teenager in southern Indiana, I hung out with the same group of guys most of the time. We went to the same school, worked for the same farmers, and spent most of our free time together. We knew each other well and generally knew what the other was thinking as he was saying it. Over the years, we had developed a way of communication that worked effectively for us. Our parents and our peers may have been confused, but we knew what we meant. For this, and probably many other reasons, we got along as only best friends could.

On occasion, this group of friends did not agree. Sometimes, we had differing opinions, and at other times we flat-out disagreed with each other. It could be about who had the fastest car, who worked harder, or what we were going to do on Saturday evening. If you were listening to these conversations, you probably would have heard something like, "Keep it up and we are going to conflict." This statement was code for "I don't agree with you." It also carried an element of humor and respect. Even with not agreeing, we respected each other enough that we knew these words were just words and at the end of the conversation or evening, we would still be best friends.

Today, as a professional, as one who has pastored churches and served in leadership roles within faith-based organizations, I find that the words "Keep it up and we are going to conflict" seemingly have a different connotation. These words seem less like respectful humor and more like a challenge or threat.

They sound like words one would use while throwing down the gauntlet and preparing for battle. The words seemingly suggest a willingness to embrace the challenge of dueling it out over anything on which we disagree.

There may be multiple reasons why this statement, as well as others like it, conjures up feelings of confrontation. From a simple perspective, we may not have the same kind of relationships with our peers or those we lead as we did with childhood friends. Perhaps and even more significantly is the fact that the issues on which we disagree are very real and potentially carry significant consequences. In addition, we may have a vested interest in protecting what we believe to be right. So, when someone says "Keep it up and we are going to conflict," those are fighting words.

As leaders, we are never going to agree with everyone, every idea someone brings to the table, or every action an individual performs. Likewise, not everyone is going to agree with everything we think and do. The reality of leadership is that we are at risk of people standing opposite us with everything from a different perspective to being adamantly opposed to something we are doing. Sometimes, it feels as though they are saying, or we are thinking, "Keep it up and we are going to conflict."

When this happens, how are we going to address it? This book will lay a foundation for how we are going to answer this question. We will spend some time understanding conflict and its nuances. The focus of this book will be on techniques for assessing and managing conflict. Throughout the book there will be many stories illustrating key points that are based on real scenarios of faith leaders. This book will help faith leaders know what to do when they feel or hear, "Keep it up and we are going to conflict."

UNDERSTANDING CONFLICT

■ He was a young pastor who had just moved to a new church. This was his second church after a couple of successful years in his first assignment. It should have been an ideal opportunity for him to grow professionally and help the church grow the kingdom. Within three months, the young pastor found himself struggling. At a recent board meeting, the church board gave him a list of things he should do and a list of things he should not do. While he was a little surprised, he took it in stride until he heard the entire list. Included in the list of things to do was requiring his wife to stay home during the day to answer the church phone. Included in the list of things he could not do was using his vacation to go hunting. There were several other similar issues on both lists.

The young pastor left that board meeting deeply disturbed and questioning his call to this particular church. On really bad days, he even questioned his call to the ministry. How could he have been so wrong in believing he was in the center of God's will? Why would God call him to a church like this? The questions continually flooded his mind and eventually the conversations he was having with his wife.

Over the next few weeks he sought counsel from trusted friends and experts who specialized in assisting clergy with difficult situations. This young pastor formulated a response to the board based on the wise counsel he received and his own perspectives about reasonable expectations. In the days leading up to the next board meeting the young pastor prayed earnestly that his response would answer the board members' questions, eliminate their concerns, and allow all of them to get on with ministry.

The day and time of the board meeting arrived. At the appropriate place in the agenda, the young pastor responded to the demands and expectations the board members laid out in their lists at the prior meeting. He gently, but emphatically, addressed their concerns issue by issue. Using every technique of effective communication he had learned, he tried to be as relational as possible but as clear as necessary. In the midst of this, he knew he needed to maintain his Christian and pastoral integrity, yet he did not want to surrender to the unreasonable expectations of the board.

Needless to say, this board meeting was a definitive moment in the relationships between that pastor, the board, and the church. While every effort had been made to bathe the meeting in prayer and every word carefully chosen, a line had been drawn. The pastor's response was not well received. The conflict had begun for this pastor, and for the most part, it defined the remaining time he served that church.

Defining Conflict

When we hear the word "conflict," we think of scenarios much like this young pastor and the church mentioned above. Generally, our minds race to a situation, circumstance, or event where two or more people are at odds with each other. Conflict usually conjures up thoughts of unfavorable circumstances. It may be ill or ill-harbored feelings toward someone or a group. Conflict may be a disagreement, sometimes a sharp disagreement, with someone. It can be the opposing view of a decision that was made or an action that was taken. Conflict can be anything that disrupts equilibrium, throwing off the harmony we sincerely seek as people of faith.

Generally speaking, the knowledge of conflict in our midst stimulates negative feelings. Our thought patterns begin to whirl around, making us wonder what went wrong and ask "what if" questions. For some, emotions go into overdrive, bouncing from faith to fear depending on what we are thinking and feeling at any given moment. The reality of conflict is often the foundation of uncertainty.

From a secular point of view, our reaction to conflict may be explained through the development of norms and mores in our society. We have been enculturated to understand conflict as disagreement, dissension, bickering, fighting, and the like. If we looked up the word "conflict" and its synonyms in a dictionary, we would discover that many of our modern-day definitions define conflict as we have above.

In a secular context, we may embrace conflict as something that happens in life. If there are people or decisions, there will be conflict. An evangelist friend of mine, who also did general contractor work, was describing concrete and how it cracks: "There are two kinds of concrete; concrete that is cracked, and concrete that is going to crack."[1] The reality of life is there is going to be conflict; if not today, in the future.

For people of faith, it may be harder to embrace this reality. We read the Scriptures, endeavor to understand them, and embrace them as precepts by which to live. We are challenged with the call to holy living that includes loving one another not only with a brotherly love but also with an agape love—a self-giving love that prefers others over self. In our finite understanding, there is a disconnect between agape love and conflict. If I love you with a self-giving love, how can I have conflict with you? If my heart is pure, how can I be at odds with a vision, a decision, a person, or anything else? If I am holy, am I not committed to seeking unity, oneness, and consensus in all things? For people of faith, accepting conflict as a reality of life is difficult if not heresy.

The truth is, conflict is going to happen, even in faith communities. As surely as concrete will crack, conflict will occur. Where there are people who have assembled together to worship or to do ministry, there will be differing opinions and perspectives. Where you have differing views, you inevitably will have conflict.

Reframing Conflict

In the church and other faith-based communities, we quickly blame conflict when things are not going well. If progress or growth is slower than hoped, we are tempted to blame it on some issue founded in conflict. When we lose a family for an unexplained reason, we want to blame a conflicted relationship with

16

the pastor or someone in the church. When finances are down, we question if someone is upset and withholding the tithe. The list goes on, but the culprit is seemingly the same—conflict.

What had the young pastor done over the three short months leading up to those board meetings that warranted the board issuing two lists of directives? Why did this pastor need to expend time and energy addressing a list of directives that seemed so unreasonable? Had he offended someone? Was he a mismatch for the church? Had he challenged the board members with something that caused them to react the way they did? The answer to these questions is a resounding "no." This young pastor had not done anything to deserve what happened. Then why did it occur?

The board's aggressive lists of directives were not personal. The church board was not reacting to something this pastor did or didn't do. The truth is, in three months the board members didn't really know him, nor he them. They were speaking from prior experiences and of times when perhaps they felt they were taken advantage of or their pastoral relationship was compromised. They were not maliciously trying to disrupt the life of this pastor, discredit his integrity, or make his life miserable. They were trying to protect their church and ensure that the pastoral relationship they hoped for would be secure.

Unfortunately, the young pastor did not interpret the church board's actions as they were intended. What felt to the board like reasonable expectations felt to the pastor like micromanaging his life and that of his family. After all, did the board really have the audacity to tell him he couldn't use his vacation to go hunting? What may have been well intentioned turned into something much different—conflict.

This church's immediate conflict was born within the time frame between two board meetings at the intersection of directives and response. The church board members probably felt they were just sharing more about their expectations. For this pastor, it was clearly an assault on the consensual contract they agreed on when he accepted the invitation to pastor the church. In addition, it felt like an encroachment on his integrity. Unfortunately, from this pastor's perspective this was a full-fledged attack and the conflict was real.

As leaders, the conflict we often sense is not directly focused on us; however, by virtue of our leadership role we find ourselves in the line of fire. Somewhere in the history of the church or organization something happened that hurt someone, compromised trust, or cast a cloud of doubt on the integrity of the leader. While people of faith should not harbor ill feelings, the memories and emotions of prior experiences impact the way people view and embrace future experiences. The truth is, the leader at the time is the one who deals with the wake.

Ironically, the church noted above may not have recognized that what just occurred at the meeting felt like an assault to the pastor and could be construed as conflict. These board members may have felt they were just being good stewards by addressing issues that they perceived to be problematic in the past. Again, it was not personal; it was just the church trying to be the church the way it perceived it needed to be. For this young pastor, he happened to be the leader and consequently bore the brunt of the confrontation.

Every leader is at risk of being engaged in conflict. Sometimes, this conflict will be such that the leader is involved personally either as the one implicated or the one who incited the conflict. Not every communication, decision, or action is going to be received with enthusiasm by everyone. Occasionally, just by the pure virtue of doing what we are called to do, someone is going to take offense and we are going to find ourselves in the midst of tension.

There will be other times when the leader is not directly involved; however, by occupying the role of the leader he or she will become part of the process to manage or resolve the conflict. People look to leadership for wisdom, guidance, and answers. While leaders know they do not have all of the answers, those who follow often think they do. People turn to faith leadership when they need support, encouragement, and assistance.

There was a strong evangelical church in an urban area that for decades was touted as one of the most sincere, authentic, evangelical churches in the community. The church was engaged in frontline ministry to the community. The parishioners were provided many opportunities for discipleship. The church was growing. By every measure, this was a great church. People in the community knew of the church, respected what it stood for, and appreciated what it did.

The time came when the long-tenured pastor retired. A new pastor was called to the church, and things appeared to be going well, at least for a while. It was soon obvious that the "honeymoon" was beginning to wear off. This great church, long known for its authenticity, was beginning to have problems. Rumors began to circulate throughout the faith community about the church's struggle to find its equilibrium with the new pastor. Some people were not happy with some of the changes being implemented. According to the rumor mill, this church was beginning to disintegrate.

It wasn't long until a small faction of people in that church started talking about other options available to them. The most logical choice to some was to pull out and start a new church. Once this group left, others began to leave the church. Some joined the new church. Several found other churches of similar faith to join. No one really knows how many left who may have ended up not going anywhere.

This great church was facing some dark days. By the time the exodus was over, many families had left the church. The faithful who remained stayed the course, but the loss of so many created undue hardships. The church had a hard time continuing all of the ministries previously offered. Morale began to decline. People in the community were talking negatively about the church. What was once a thriving church was now a church surviving the aftermath of conflict.

What happened? How could such a great church suffer so much? What could be so horrible that it would cause a mass exodus of people? Did someone do something intentionally to sabotage the church? Did the people overreact? Was the new pastor the wrong pastor? The list of questions goes on and on.

The reality is everyone believed he or she was doing the right thing. The long-tenured pastor felt it was time to retire. The new pastor was leading with confidence and conviction. The people felt their expectations were appropriate. When the time came for some of the people to leave the church, they left feeling as if they should either help start the new church or go to another church. The bottom line is everyone believed he or she was doing the right thing at the time he or she did it, and yet it resulted in what was perceived as conflict.

This church suffered immensely. The new pastor ended up leaving the church in just a few years. The church struggled with resourcing ministries. Finances were tight. The reputation of the church had been compromised. Yet one could hypothesize that no one did anything that was ill willed.

The moral of this story is people are not always ill intentioned. As a rule, parishioners are not strategically planning how to stir up a hornet's nest or plotting how to hurt a pastor. Likewise, leaders are not scheming on how to demoralize their followers. Generally speaking, leaders and their followers are well intentioned. They are looking out for what they believe to be in the best interest of all involved. The issue is that diverse opinions do not always align with what individuals believe to be in their own best interest or that of the church. When this happens, conflict can occur.

Conflict as Opportunity

It is important for faith leaders to understand that conflict does not necessarily have to be a negative. We do not have to run and hide, nor do we need to prepare for battle. Dr. Charles Perabeau, professor of sociology at Olivet Nazarene University and a bivocational pastor, says, "Conflict may be viewed as opportunity. It does not have to be a bad thing; it can be something from which good can come."[2] As faith leaders, we want and need to change the lens through which we see conflict.

Two leaders had worked together informally for approximately five years. Their relationship was collegial and professional. They had a few lunch meetings together, discussed similar professional ventures, and genuinely had an interest in the well-being of the organization with which both were affiliated. There were even conversations of hope that they could work jointly on a major project someday.

One day, one of the leaders was part of a committee that was making decisions about who would be assigned to what task groups in the organization. These appointments would be driven by a multitude of factors, including skill set, content knowledge, and interpersonal relationship skills. The committee was taking very seriously who would be assigned to what group assignment. It wanted a group who could effectively complete the task and who could work together well. Every committee member weighed in with his or her perspective and expectation about the group assignments. Each member also identified who would best serve which group.

When the committee meeting was over, the other leader who was not part of the committee ended up not being assigned to a group. When the assignments were announced, he was devastated. He fully expected to be in a lead role, if not leading one of the groups. At first he was calm, but as time passed, it began to bother him considerably. In a moment of extreme frustration, he accused the committee members of not recognizing his ability, devaluing him, and hindering his ability to make a more significant contribution to the organization. None of this was true, but it was the way he saw the decision. It became very personal for him.

As time passed, opportunity presented itself for the two leaders to discuss what happened openly and honestly. The one who was not assigned expressed his hurt and disappointment. He said that he felt underappreciated and at times used. The one who served on the committee shared how the process unfolded and how the committee arrived at its decisions. While both leaders had different perspectives, each was willing to be open minded and hear the other's view. When the leader who was not assigned understood the complete process and rationale, he acknowledged his conclusions were in error. He recognized that it was not personal and that the committee was just taking seriously the work it was charged to do.

Many times conflict provides a framework for seeing a situation through a different lens. We may have looked at a program, a ministry, or a person one way for years. Then something happens that forces us to think, see, or act differently. When this occurs, we have a choice. We can call this difference conflict, or we can embrace the difference as an opportunity. It really is a matter of perspective.

When we move beyond seeing conflict as only a negative from which we anticipate negative outcomes to seeing it as an opportunity, we can more likely anticipate positive outcomes. They will be different for sure. We will think differently. We will see things differently. It may even change the way we do what we do. In the end, we will have capitalized on making the most out of what was before us. Conflict can be the driving force that moves us to doing something spectacular.

Conflicted circumstances contain opportunities to demonstrate grace and compassion, reflect Christ's character, and model Christian behavior. Rather than viewing conflict as a negative situation in which we must engage for better or worse, we can reframe it and see it as an opportunity to effect positive change. Through the attitude and actions of the leader, conflict can be managed in a way that hopefully creates a win for everyone involved.

Leaders will find themselves in the midst of conflicted situations. It is part of the job! How we view it and what we do with it will define our leadership. If we react with negative emotion and actions, the conflict will fit the definition of our popular culture. If we act with Christlike character and grounded wisdom, we can reframe the conflict and make it the next opportunity on the horizon.

ASSESSING CONFLICT

■ A young pastor was in his first church as pastor. He believed that God had called him to this church, and he worked tirelessly in tandem with the church leaders to build the church. From weekly evangelistic visitation to sprucing up the facilities, there wasn't anything this pastor wouldn't do. For the first eighteen months of his ministry things went well. A few individuals were added to the congregation, ministries were started, and the facilities were being updated. From every indication, this pastor was having an effective ministry.

What this pastor did not know when he accepted the church, but began to learn very early, was that this church had a troubled history. This church had a reputation in the community. Unfortunately, it was not a good reputation. Yes, he knew the church had been closed previously, two times to be exact, and reopened twice. He knew the church had lost a lot of people who now attended other denominations. He knew the current congregation was relatively new to the church and in some cases new to faith. What he was learning was just how much baggage the church carried.

The neighbors who had been in the neighborhood for any time at all would tell the pastor about incidents when something specific happened. One individual gave an account about the romantic affair that had occurred between certain members of the leadership and how it seemed so inappropriate. Another neighbor recounted the day there was a "big fistfight" on the lawn after church. Rumors existed about church leadership committing illegal acts. Story after story, it became apparent that this church had a sordid past.

What this pastor soon discovered was the current members and attendees were committed and faithful, but the baggage this church carried was weighing the church down in the community. The more the pastor and the church leaders tried to connect and reach out, the more they learned and the more embarrassed they became. No matter how hard they tried, it just seemed they could not overcome the stigma of yesteryear.

It wasn't long until the morale of the faithful began to suffer. It seemed that every time the church tried to reach out, invest, and make a difference, it was confronted with apathy, suspicion, and cynicism. It became clear that the neighborhood did not trust the church or its people. The church leaders felt they were swimming upstream against the current. Even though they believed in the power of God, they were losing hope that this church could be the church they envisioned and wanted.

At approximately the eighteenth-month mark in the tenure of this pastor, the church faithful decided that they needed to do something different. They had given the last few years to trying to make this church strong, but to no avail. At a regularly scheduled meeting of the church board, the leaders, with tears in their eyes, informed the pastor that they had collectively decided to move on and find a church where they could experience fruit from their labor.

Needless to say, this young pastor was devastated. He had poured his heart and soul into trying to make the church dynamic. He genuinely loved the people and enjoyed serving them. At the same time, he felt their pain and discouragement. In some ways, he didn't blame them for arriving at this decision. Questions raced through his mind. How could the church continue if all of the leadership made a mass exodus? What would others think about his pastoral leadership? What new stories would the community have to tell?

The young pastor contacted his district supervisory leader to share what was happening and seek counsel. The immediate reaction and quick conclusion of this supervisor was that this pastor must have done something wrong and that there was conflict in the midst. The leader arranged for a meeting with the church leadership. The meeting occurred as planned with all of the church leaders attending. The district leader led the meeting with grace and poise but with suspicion that the evening would eventually turn to mediation between the church leaders and this young pastor.

As the meeting ensued, the church leaders were in agreement; the issue was not with the pastor. They articulated that they were just tired of trying so hard only to be viewed as outcasts in the community. They no longer wanted to keep expending energy to no avail. They were ready to move on and get involved in a church where they could make a difference. They wanted to go to a church that was respected and where they did not have to be embarrassed every time they told what church they attended. They wanted to raise their families in a healthy church. By the end of the evening, the district leader acknowledged his bias coming into the meeting and his new understanding of the situation. He acknowledged his appreciation for the church leaders and what they had tried to do. The meeting ended in concerted prayer.

By the end of the month, all of the key leaders were gone, and the rest of the small congregation followed. The district leader officially acknowledged the church as inactive and assisted the young pastor in finding another ministry opportunity. The church was later officially closed, and the facilities sold.

Understanding the Conflict

The young pastor above sincerely appreciated the support and encouragement of the church leadership and of his supervisor. It was refreshing and encouraging that he was not the one being blamed for the exodus of the people or the status of the church. On the other hand, he was still perplexed. Why would God call him to this church to see this kind of saga unfold? Is there something else he could have done? What really happened?

The truth is, the events and circumstances of the past were out of the control of this pastor. He could not erase the memories of those in the community who remembered isolated incidents when the church did not act like the church. Even though he loved the church people and tried his best to minister to them, he could not dictate how they felt or how they responded to circumstances. In some ways, everyone was a victim of circumstances beyond individual control.

Whenever a leader is trying to understand an ongoing incident or event, he or she must look at all sides of the issue. Leaders must perform a good assessment to understand what is really happening from every perspective possible. Jumping to conclusions, making assumptions, and responding reactively are sure ways to misread a situation and end up making a wrong conclusion. For a leader, the failure to perform a good assessment means running the risk of hurting others or having his or her leadership viewed as ineffective.

Wise leaders become information and data gatherers. When an incident or situation is occurring, a wise leader gathers as much information about the situation as possible. Likewise, if the decision involves any kind of data, the leader will want to collect and analyze this data to help guide the decision-making process. Too many decisions are made with limited knowledge or without all of the facts. Wise leaders will make sure they do not fall prey to making decisions with limited facts.

One of the greatest ways to understand what is happening is to use a model from the social sciences commonly referred to as the ecological perspective. This model looks at the relationships, connections, and influencers that are part of a person's life or a situation. The premise is that all of us are shaped by our environment, culture, and history. Looking at a situation through this lens helps us see the conflicted issue from different angles and have a better understanding about what is occurring.

28

A quick ecological look at the church described above demonstrated the church was living in an environment where people in the community did not respect it and generally devalued it. Culturally, the community was apathetic to the church. The history of the church included not only memories of incidents and rumors of inappropriate behaviors but also its having been closed and reopened twice. These things alone could partially explain why the church's leadership was ready to move on to another church.

The fact of the matter is, every person and institution is influenced by these broad categories. People and their context are interrelated and interdependent. Who I am will be largely influenced by the environment in which I was raised, the culture to which I was exposed, and the historical markers that impacted my life. A person born and raised in affluence will interpret things different from a person born and raised in poverty. Living through a tragedy will cause a person to see things different from a person who has never experienced that tragedy. A person raised with a Christian worldview will see life different from someone who has never been introduced to Christ.

Faith leaders need to think about this ecological model as they attempt to understand the conflict in their midst. What is happening environmentally? Are there political or economic factors influencing those involved in the conflict? What dynamics are in play socially? What impact do systems such as institutions and laws have on the situation? What are the views influencing the way people were raised and taught the norms and mores of society? Understanding the environmental context will help the leader have greater insight into the conflict.

Culturally, leaders want to understand those things that predefine attitudes and behaviors. What traditions and customs exist in an organization, church, or community? What are the general attitudes toward life itself and the standard and quality of living? What are the accepted values, norms, and mores that guide the culture in the organization, church, or community? What are the usual problem-solving skills exercised in times of conflict. Answering these questions can help a leader better ascertain how the culture influences views and prompts responses to conflict.

Leaders should never discount the power of historical memory and the impact of significant events on a person's life. These things can influence and motivate people to respond in certain ways because they remember how things were. Such defining events can have a profound effect on the way people view the present. Someone who lived through World War II and experienced the rationing of needed resources may hoard such resources just in case something similar happens again. The lives of people are forever changed by those defining life moments. Understanding a person's historical context will give us insight into understanding the conflicted situation better.

Influencers to Conflict

Circumstances and situations are influenced by a vast array of internal and external factors. Creeds, statements of faith, familial ties, status, history, culture, environment, and so much more, directly affect the way people see and experience events and circumstances. Every organization was started with a passion, driven by a purpose, and governed by people to address a problem or meet a need. All of these factors shaped and formed the church or organization as we know it.

Familial ties run deep. These include not only the relationships in immediate or extended families but also those that people have built with one another, especially in the church. When one hurts, many hurt. When one is offended, others are offended. When someone is wronged, several may be willing to take up the fight on that person's behalf. Family members may have the tendency to view, think, act, and respond in similar ways. Wise leaders should never forget the power of relationships between those whom they serve.

Organizations have individuals who rise from within to assume roles of leadership. In an ideal environment, these are people whose hearts are transformed and who lead transformationally. These are the lay leaders and employees who model and exemplify the attitudes, behaviors, and decision-making attributes of authentic Christian servant leadership. Unfortunately, not everyone in leadership carries all of these attributes. Sometimes those in leadership influence and confuse the issues to the point that they stir up issues and possibly incite conflict. Faith leaders need to be cognizant of this.

Most institutions will have governance documents. Churches will have statements of faith, denominational manuals, bylaws, or some other type of similar document that defines who they are and what they do. Organizations will have vision and mission statements accompanied with bylaws, and possibly other types of documents, to describe who they are and what they do. In both cases, governance structures influence what institutions do. If people do not completely agree with the adopted documents, it can cause conflict.

For the church, we are seeing a transition taking place in the way we worship and the focus of that worship. Many people are no longer choosing churches based on doctrine. These individuals are looking for churches where they feel emotionally moved and where they can build relationships. The postmodern culture's influence on churches has pointed us to different worship styles, trends, and expectations. The more widespread this becomes, the less of a role tradition and doctrine will play. While we are thankful for those who attend our churches, our churches are melting pots of beliefs, values, and mores. This kind of context makes the possibility of conflict even greater.

All organizations reside in a community. Every community has its own culture. This culture reflects the generally held values, norms, and mores of that community. Even if the organization we serve intends to be different, the people who attend worship at our organization or are employed or served by it will mirror the culture of the broader community. Depending on where we serve and what we do, the culture of the organization can be different. This can create a context where our organization feels the pressures of a countercultural environment.

There are many things that can influence conflict in our organizations. Any one of them could be significant and cause issues that we need to respond to as leaders. The truth is, there are probably more than just one of these at work at the same time. For example, we may have a strong lay leader in our church that represents a prominent family in the community. This individual may have grown up in the community and been acculturated with community values and norms. The church, on the other hand, may possess a value system that runs counter to the culture of the community at large. So, now we have a leader whose community and family ties are deep and whose value system is similar to that of the surrounding community. This individual is providing leadership in an institution where his values may not be aligned with those of the institution. This can result in conflict.

The fact of the matter is, every leader will face situations influenced by many factors. There will be a dynamic tension between the organization and those internal and external forces that influence the organization. The good news is that most will not result in conflict. As leaders, we understand the dynamic and adapt accordingly. The key is being aware. We need to understand the organization and the community where we serve. Likewise, we need to perform a good assessment to understand what is really influencing our organization and community.

Stressors to Conflict

We have organizations that are influenced by many internal and external factors of which we need to be aware. We also need to be cognizant of those incidents, situations, and circumstances that randomly occur and add additional stress. Using the example above in which the church leader was part of a prominent family in the community, a local company going out of business could have a profound impact on that leader's extended family and the community at large. This leader could bring that stress to the church board meeting and make a financial decision for the church while feeling that stress. The decision could be right, or it could be wrong. However, the motivation for it may have been driven by a stressor rather than divine direction.

Leaders face these kinds of scenarios often. There are acts, events, decisions, relationships, and more, that stimulate stress for individuals, organizations, and communities. When this happens, the stress may be brought to worship or work. It influences the way people think and act. Stressful incidents may cause people to do things they would not normally do and things the leader would not normally expect.

Conflict often originates when situations or circumstances, already influenced by multiple factors, are impacted by additional stressors. This impact is enough that it disrupts equilibrium and causes an imbalance to the homeostatic state. When this occurs, we react. Periodically, the reactions are such that they lead to conflicted situations in which something or someone becomes the target.

With both influencers and stressors, leaders need to ascertain those things that are impacting their organizations. No two organizations will be influenced by identical indicators, and no two will experience the exact same outcomes from stressors. On the other hand, all organizations will find themselves acting and reacting to those things that influence their cultures and add stress. Leaders, by performing a good assessment and staying continuously alert to the changing landscape, can be aware of what is happening. When the outcome is conflict, the leader will have a better idea of why it occurred. This in turn will help the leader know how to respond.

FRAMING CONFLICT

A long-established urban church was experiencing a wave of growth, excitement, outreach, and more. In the two most recent years, the church had nearly doubled its attendance, done major remodeling, started new ministries, and, most importantly, saw people come to know the Lord. Things were looking good, feeling good, and going well. It was a time in the life of the church with which most were pleased and excited.

As great as things were, the church was still not perfect. The church was working really hard to add value to the Sunday school program. People would come to worship and to attend other events and activities, but Sunday school was just holding its own. The church was trying to use Sunday school to serve as the primary opportunity for children's ministry, youth small groups, and adult discipleship. While Sunday school was not the only venue for these things, it was the main focus.

An issue arose that turned into conflict. One of the church leaders, a board member to be exact, decided that he could contribute more to the life of the church if instead of going to Sunday school, he walked the neighborhoods placing tracts on people's doors. Without fanfare or notice, he started missing Sunday school. It was soon learned that he was busy carrying out his neighborhood outreach plan, going door-to-door, passing out tracts, and inviting people to Sunday school and church. Admirable! Paradoxical?

This gentleman's passion for the lost was obvious. He so desired to see people come to a saving knowledge of Christ that he would do just about anything to share the gospel with someone. He gave up evenings and weekends to serve others. He bought his own tracts in bulk. He prayed earnestly. He would talk to anyone and bring the conversation around to knowing Jesus. Honestly, you had to admire his intensity and commitment.

When he started missing Sunday school to pass out tracts, it just seemed so counterintuitive. He was a strong part of the church, a board member, and a leader. He understood the emphasis of the church's initiative on getting people to Sunday school and spoke favorably of the same. It just seemed quite paradoxical that he would elect to miss Sunday school to invite people to Sunday school and church.

The pastor tried to assess the situation and evaluate the results of what was happening. On the one hand, he appreciated the man's enthusiasm and passion to reach out to the community. On the other hand, the pastor wondered how the church could demonstrate commitment and add value to Sunday school if the church leaders did not participate. If the value of this man's evangelistic efforts during Sunday school was greater, then how do you explain it to others who may be less interested in Sunday school? It was a difficult situation for the pastor to understand and address.

Eventually, the pastor did address the issue with the gentleman. Both were kind and gracious. The man explained his passion, concern, and commitment for reaching others. The pastor explained his concerns and his commitment to Sunday school. He also asked the parishioner to reevaluate what he was doing and see if there was another time it could be done. The pastor even volunteered to go with him if he did it at another time. The conversation ended without immediate resolution, but it was on the horizon. The man continued to miss Sunday school to evangelize the community for a few more weeks, then returned to Sunday school.

Motivational Forces

Virtually every side of conflict has a motivational force that is driving it. Generally speaking, these forces are grounded in the ecological influencers of environment, culture, and history. Built on these influencers are specific indicators such as beliefs, perspectives, convictions, and opinions. The man above believed there was more value to him passing out tracts than there was to attending Sunday school. His commitment to evangelizing others was more important to him than his own personal discipleship or that which he would add to a class discussion.

These motivational forces are powerful. They are the foundations on which people frame opinions, pass judgments, and make decisions. They are the context for how people view situations. They provide meaning or explanation to circumstances. They can be perceived as positive and of great value. They also can be viewed as negative and delivering a spirit of dissension and division. They are the perceptions that drive a sense of reality. Right or wrong, they frame the way people see, act, and react to what is occurring around them and especially to them.

There are some things that are common to groups of people. Generally speaking, faith-based organizations lean toward a biblical worldview. This framework of understanding will be built on the foundations of the Bible; however, there may be nuances that are minor in the grand scheme of faith and Christian living. Within the faith-based context, there is a certain comfort level with holding on to these views. Outside of the faith-based context, these views may be countercultural and create circumstances that are uncomfortable or even rife with conflict.

As leaders attempt to assess conflict, these motivational forces will come into play. In some cases, they will make sense and be self-explanatory as one looks at the ecology of the person or issue. At other times, the motivational forces will be less obvious but nevertheless very real. It is important for the leader to understand these forces and the dynamic they have on the situation at hand.

Two faith-based organizations could be experiencing similar situations. Both could perform good assessments and determine what the real issue is at hand. As the leaders ascertain who is involved and begin to develop a plan for addressing the issue, they may learn that motivations are totally different. In one situation, a man may miss Sunday school and pass out tracts because of his commitment to evangelism. The other situation may be a man missing Sunday school and passing out tracts because it's a reasonable activity in lieu of attending a class where he cannot tolerate the teacher. These are similar issues with two different motivational forces.

It is imperative that a faith leader work to understand the motivations behind the conflicted situations in which he or she is dealing. In some cases, this will be easier to do. People may be extremely verbal, or the motivation is obvious. In other situations, it will be very difficult. A leader may never really know the true motivations or know them completely; however, to the best of his or her ability a leader must strive to understand. Only through understanding can a leader truly know how to address conflict.

Many churches face similar difficult situations: spiritual maturity levels of leadership, finances, physical resources, leadership styles, resistance to change, worship-style preferences, and more. While these present common problems, the truth is, every church faces them in a different environment, in a different culture, and with a different history. When conflicts arise, the motivational forces driving the conflict may be different. A pastor cannot assume the same problem another church is having is the exact same in his or her church. It may seem the same, but the motivations may be different. Consequently, it should be handled differently.

Strengths Perspective

A helpful process for assessing and reframing conflict is to look for the strengths in the people and circumstances. Every person, regardless of his or her position in the conflict, will have some qualities and attributes that should be recognized. The gentleman above had several strengths in spite of his missing Sunday school: he was evangelistic, he was committed to outreach, and he invited people to church. Even though he was creating a conflicted situation for the pastor, the man had many great qualities that needed to be acknowledged.

Most situations have positive indicators and outcomes although the overall situation may feel negative. Again, the situation above included several strengths: people were receiving tracts with the gospel message, someone from the church was reaching out, and the church was being advertised. While the timing and rationale may not have suited the pastor, the outcomes could be perceived as positive.

When we are facing conflict, too many times we see only the negative side of the issue. Our tendency is to look for those things that are wrong or potentially offer adverse consequences. We are tempted to see only the bad attitudes, negative feelings, opposite opinions, or other undesirable features. Reframing the situation using a strengths perspective enables us to see past the negatives and identify the positives.

It is the strengths of a situation that give us a foundation on which to begin creative planning and intervention. If the only perspective we see is the negative, we will spend a lot of creative energy trying to overcome the barriers and problems. If we can identify the strengths, we can channel that creative energy into building an intervention plan that builds on those strengths and those things that are positive. Conflict management is much easier when we are working with what is right instead of just what is wrong.

Systems Thinking

For a leader to truly manage conflict, he or she must think about how the situation or issue is affecting the whole organization. This is thinking in systems. A change, alteration, or adjustment to one part of the organization can have a ripple effect through the entire organization. The man who passed out tracts instead of attending Sunday school had an impact on the church. People knew he was not attending. His spouse and children were answering questions about his absence. His action was impacting the whole body.

Systems thinking acknowledges that an issue may have an impact on the whole organization even if just one person is involved. One incident or event can cause a tremble throughout the organization. Likewise, an intervention can have the same effect, if not more severe. In some cases, an organization may have learned to live with a certain amount of dysfunction caused by a conflicted situation. Applying an intervention may be too much for the organization to absorb without there being additional and significant implications.

Sometimes the conflict an organization is facing has more than one force fueling it. There may be many factors that are converging to stimulate the conflict. Parsons and Leas state, "Systemic thinking assumes multiple causes—not a single cause; it assumes that there are many contributing factors to any given set of circumstances."[1] Generally speaking, as we perform an assessment, we can identify the ecological factors that are in play. Often we can identify the influencers and stressors that are weighing on the conflict. Generally it is not as simple as finding one little thing to address. Instead, it is a conglomerate of factors creating stress that leads to the conflict.

When managing conflict, leaders need to think about the whole—the system of the organization. Even if it appears that only one person is involved or the incident appears to be an isolated event, leaders need to think about how the whole organization is being affected. In some cases, the effect may be minor. In others, the effect could be significant. It is the leader's job to assess this and, to the degree possible, protect the system.

The caveat with systems thinking is not to let conflict get out of control by making it more than it needs to be. Even when the system is being affected, if the conflict can be contained and managed on a smaller scale, it should be done. The more public conflict becomes, the more difficult it will be to address. It is like the old adage "Don't make a mountain out of a mole-hill"; that is, don't make something more out of an issue just because you are thinking about the systemic impact.

When applying systems thinking to the church, it is reasonable to think of the system as a family. Family Systems Theory suggests that congregations behave like families.[2] Most families develop a state of homeostasis. Members learn each other's idiosyncrasies, how to anticipate and react to them, and how to manage them when necessary. They develop communication patterns and coping skills and create their own norms. Families are resilient and find ways of managing conflict that work for them. Probably more than any other system, they love and accept each other. In some ways, the church is like this. Leaders of churches need to think about conflict management from a family perspective.

When we think in systems, we think about conflict management in ways that have us seeking the best interest of the whole. This means conflict management is more than tackling a specific problem or individual without regard for the ultimate outcome. Conflict management may be limited to an isolated situation or one person, but the systemic impact is given strong consideration.

A faith-based, not-for-profit organization found itself needing to terminate an employee for a breach of ethical conduct. The organization's employee handbook was clear: any employee committing such a breach would be terminated immediately. The executive director facilitated the termination knowing it would create some challenges for the organization. He also knew he had to do it to maintain the integrity of the organization and the intent of the board of directors as outlined in the employee handbook.

The ripple effect was major. The employee had nurtured many strong relationships with several people affiliated with the organization. A few of them were instantly angry and severed their relationships with the organization. A few of them directed their anger at the executive director and blamed him for the problem. Some of them even went as far as to say things such as, "We thought this was a Christian organization." One person continued his relationship with the organization but held the executive director at a distance and refused to do some of the things he once did.

To complicate matters, the individual who was terminated continued to socialize with some of the people. For the executive director, it felt as though someone kept rubbing salt into a wound. It would burn and produce pain, reminding everyone of what happened. Occasionally, conversations would ensue around the organization about how great that person was or how unjust it was that the individual was let go.

The executive director did what had to be done, but the systemic impact was significant. He made the decision based on the system's guidelines established by the governing body. While the systemic ripple would be difficult to control with those who had close relationships with this employee, the executive director was protecting the system. Sometimes systemic thinking is about the greater good even when there will be other systemic implications.

Conflict management is a challenging task for most leaders. This challenge becomes more manageable when leaders understand motivational forces driving conflicted situations, identify the strengths on which an intervention can be built, and think about the systemic impact to minimize risk for the greater good. If a leader can understand why someone is doing what he or she is doing and then acknowledge the strengths within it, that leader can make decisions that not only serve those involved but also protect the whole.

MANAGING CONFLICT

■ An executive director of a faith-based organization had to fire an employee for gross negligence of her duties. It was a difficult situation. She had only worked at the organization for less than a year. The employee presented well, appeared competent, and sounded enthusiastic about embracing the challenges of the job position. She started well, and every indication was that she was going to do well.

A few months into employment several other employees in the organization were starting to express concern. The executive director had noticed that some things were not getting accomplished, deadlines were being missed, and, most importantly, people were not being served with the commitment to excellence the agency purported. There were gaps in what the agency said and what was happening. Every indicator pointed back to this employee.

The executive director met with the employee on multiple occasions to sort out some of the issues and encourage her to focus her attention on what she should be doing. Each time, the employee agreed to step it up and make sure she was fulfilling her responsibilities. These kinds of conversations occurred frequently over a period of several months. Every time the executive director thought it was resolved, something else would occur to create another issue.

One day the executive director received a call from an external source expressing great concern about a situation. As he assessed what happened, he learned that this employee had not fulfilled certain commitments on behalf of the agency. To complicate the matter, multiple families the agency served were adversely affected. By the time the agency resolved the issues with the families and fulfilled the commitments, the agency had invested a substantial amount of staff time and financial resources.

The situation did not bode well for the employee. It was decided that the negligence was not a matter of a learning curve in which time and experience would make a difference. Rather, the negligence was a lack of work ethic and commitment. The executive director felt he had no option but to terminate the employee. He confronted her, laid out the facts, and provided a severance package to assist her as she transitioned into a job somewhere else.

Handling Conflict

There are not any easy answers for how to handle conflict. There is not a "one size fits all" solution that can be applied in every situation. Every conflicted issue is different and will require a leader to use different skills and ultimately make different decisions. Knowing what to do, when to do it, and how to do it is what makes managing conflict challenging.

There are some conflicted situations where church or organizational policy will dictate. Many organizations have thorough employee handbooks, codes of conduct, or a code of ethics that outlines what should happen when a certain type of misconduct or breach of ethic occurs. Many churches have polity manuals or other documents that outline what happens in certain situations. In both cases, a leader who is faced with a conflicted situation described in one of these documents has no choice but to practice due diligence and follow procedure.

Some leaders try to circumvent the policies to serve their own needs or lessen the impact on the organization. When this happens, the organization suffers. Not following through on written policy usurps the integrity of the organization and will ultimately discredit the organization's reputation. Leaders need to be diligent in upholding policy and following through. It is not always easy, but it must be done.

An organization's decision-making culture may define how conflicted situations are managed. Organizations that have an authoritarian style of governance may rely on the leader to handle the conflict. He or she may do all of the assessment, initiate intervention, and ultimately be responsible to bring about a resolution. In this kind of culture, the conflict tends to be kept more personal, and hopefully, only those involved are truly aware of the details. The leader is trusted to manage the process and facilitate a solution that is in the best interest of all involved.

In organizations where the culture is much more congregational, the practice may be to lean on a committee, board, or task group to work through the conflict. There may be a standing committee, that is, a grievance committee, whose sole responsibility is to deal with conflicted situations. This kind of structure does offer some benefits. It keeps the leader from being solely responsible, and by involving more people, it allows for the collective wisdom of the group. The downside is more people are privy to the details, which increases the risk of the conflict's escalation or a breach of confidentiality.

There are some organizations that have a blended style of governance. In these organizations the work and responsibility may be shared between leadership and a committee or board. This model also lets more people know about the conflict; however, it does allow for the collective wisdom of the group with the leader's input and expertise. It also insulates the leader from being the sole person blamed for the outcome.

Organizations have a tendency to handle conflict based on their ideological foundations or theological frameworks. Some organizations have adopted an ideology in which conflict is essentially seen as sinful. No matter the circumstances, causes, or consequences, conflict is viewed as wrong and should be avoided. Organizations that hold this belief typically respond to conflict in one of two ways. The first response is to pretend it does not exist. Unless something is so significant that it cannot be ignored, this ideology sweeps it away and goes on as though nothing is happening. The other response is much more dramatic. It involves identifying the person or persons responsible and essentially dismissing them or even excommunicating them, because sin in their lives is causing problems for the organization.

This ideology is inherent with risk, especially from a spiritual perspective. Norman Shawchuck states, "When the church ignores or suppresses conflict, it may be hindering the work of Christ within the congregation. When pastors teach that conflict in the congregation is sinful, they may be hindering the work of the Spirit."[1] By pretending the conflict does not exist or removing those who are responsible for the conflict from our midst, we risk not seeing the power of God work in the hearts and lives of those who may need it most.

On the other end of the spectrum is an ideology that is nearly as detrimental. This is the perspective that conflict is going to occur and should be embraced as a normal part of relationships and a norm for the culture of the organization. Leaders may purport, "It is going to occur, so let it happen." While conflict is inevitable, it cannot be permitted to run rampant. If it does, it only helps sustain the culture of conflict. An organization that is known for its culture of conflict will compromise its testimony in the eyes of those whose ideology believes faith-based organizations should love one another and live in unity.

A third ideology is one that is somewhere between the previous two. It also recognizes that conflict is inevitable; however, it embraces conflict as an opportunity. This ideology works through varying opinions, ideas, or disagreements and finds an agreeable outcome with which everyone involved can live. It does not dismiss conflict, pretend it doesn't exist, discount those responsible, or hinder the work of the Spirit. It rises to the challenge of finding a peaceful and productive resolution.

Preparation for Conflict

Leaders who desire to build a culture of healthy conflict management will want to build the capacity for it. This begins by helping those in their organizations understand conflict management and how to approach it. Leaders should strive to create a culture where conflict is embraced as an opportunity to take something seemingly negative and turn it into a positive.

One of the best ways to build capacity is to teach followers how to respond when they are faced with a conflicted situation. In churches, pastoral leadership may want to spend time teaching scriptural principles on the value of relationships, forgiveness, oneness, injustice, righteous anger, and more.[2] For church employees and in nonchurch organizations, leaders may want to provide professional development or lead conversations about conflict management with staff.

Organizations that have policies may have guidelines for how conflict is handled. While these policies are important, they often address only the major infractions of illegal and immoral activity as deemed by the organization. An organization that is serious about building capacity for conflict management may elect to further develop guidelines and protocols. There is no way every possible issue that could ever come up can be addressed, but an organization can be better prepared with principles, procedures, and processes that will serve as a foundation.

Leaders should take it upon themselves to do their own professional development in managing conflict. The more a leader understands about conflict, the dynamics of conflicted relationships, and the basic principles for dealing with conflict, the more prepared that leader will be to manage conflict when it occurs. Having the ability to assess situations and identify influencers and stressors, along with the know-how to intervene, will benefit the leader immensely.

People look to leadership for guidance, help, and answers. Leaders need to have enough knowledge, skill, and experience to engage in conflict management without making matters worse. Without being arrogant, leaders need a confidence in their own ability to assess, understand, and begin leading conflict management processes. Preparation of the leader is a good capacity-building strategy. Modeling healthy attitudes and actions will be the best teacher of all.

Leaders can help build capacity by ensuring the organization is being true to its vision, mission, and values. When the purposes of the organization are being honored and fulfilled, the organization is being true to itself. Two things happen: people have a vested interest in making sure the organization is fulfilling its mission instead of being easily led astray; situations that contradict the mission become obvious and are somewhat easier to address.

The Scriptures declare, "Where there is no vision, the people perish" (Prov. 29:18a, KJV). People without a vision will focus on petty, mundane, or selfish ambitions. Without a guiding vision, people will wander all over the place looking for something that is worthy of their creative energy. If it is not the mission, then it will be something else. The more focused people are on the vision and mission, the less likely they are to get distracted by something else.

One more aspect of building capacity has to do with building healthy relationships in an organization. Dr. Mark Quanstrom, pastor, author, and professor, stated, "The quality of fellowship, separate from tasks in the church, is so important. It is harder for destructive conflict to arise if people like each other."[3] Dr. Quanstrom's comment is true for any institution. Leaders should strive to see healthy relationships develop within their organization. The goal is to create an atmosphere of authentic love and caring for one another. When this happens, it will be harder for people to be in conflict.

Building capacity is a key component in preparing to manage conflict. It really does come down to the five ideas outlined above: (1) training our constituencies, (2) developing foundational guidelines and protocols, (3) the professional development of the leader, (4) keeping the organization focused on vision and mission, and (5) creating genuine relationships. Leaders who embrace a preparedness plan for conflict management with these five components will be far more ready to face conflict.

Managing the Conflict

Every leader, regardless of how much he or she has done to build capacity, will eventually face a situation or circumstance that will require him or her to engage in conflict management. After assessing the conflict, considering the systemic implications, and making a decision to intervene, a leader needs to know how to intervene. How can the conflict be managed in a way that brings positive resolution and preserves the integrity, dignity, and worth of all those involved?

As stated, every conflicted situation or issue is different. While we will find circumstantial similarities and parallel thought processes, each incident will be unique and require its own response. Each incident will have different people involved who will think, act, and react differently. No two conflicted situations are exactly the same—even if it feels as though they are. This will mandate the leader to be well versed in intervention techniques and flexible enough to use different approaches.

Shawchuck and Heuser state, "Church conflicts are often habitual and escalate into ever tightening cycles of destructive behavior."[4] Conflict that goes unmanaged can create a powerful negative force in an organization. This force becomes stronger the longer it goes. It furrows its way deeper into the heart and soul of the organization compromising the core purposes and values of the organization. Wise leaders know this and will work to manage the conflict to minimize adverse consequences.

Sometimes a leader may start to intervene in conflict only to learn more information or discover the chosen intervention isn't working. Norma Cook Everist suggests conflict has fluidity.[5] It is dynamic. It changes even while it is happening. What we think we knew may not be everything there is to know. As we move through conflict, it is possible that tidbits of information may surface, the focus of the conflict may be redirected, or the intervention may be deflected. Any number of natural reactions to intervention can occur and often will. Consequently, leaders need to be prepared for whatever may come.

There are two things to keep in mind when planning a conflict intervention. First of all, there are the personal relationships of those involved.[6] The relationships that exist are critically important. We noted that building healthy relationships is one way to build capacity. Preserving those relationships is incredibly important for ongoing conflict management.

It is too easy when conflict occurs for people to dismiss relationships for the principles of the conflict. Even Christians, as sincere as they may be, find that conflict has a way of eroding the relationships they value and once held dear. Keeping a priority on relationships will keep the conflict management focused. It will help those involved prioritize what really is important.

Second, it is important to remember the goals and objectives of those involved in the conflict.[7] It is also easy for leaders to jump to conclusions about the attitudes and behaviors of those who are inciting what is perceived to be conflict. Everyone who challenges a statement, disagrees with a decision, or resists something new may not be ill willed. He or she may just not have enough information or have caught the vision yet. Generally speaking, people are not vicious or vindictive; they are just committed to their beliefs and values.

Wise leaders recognize the value and blessing of people being willing to express themselves even when they are disagreeing. It is not always about an attack on leadership. It may be an affirmation of wanting to do the right thing, with someone feeling the right thing to be something else. David Lieberman states, "We argue over the right to be heard, the right to have our beliefs validated, and the right to be who we are."[8] Leaders need to be gracious, compassionate, and open minded. Using good assessment, leaders need to look at the heart of a person and see the intent.

Conflict Management Model

There are several models for dealing with conflict.[9] The next six chapters of this book lay out what is called the Six Cs Model of conflict management. This is really a framework for understanding how and when to use certain approaches to manage the conflict at hand. There are six options. Leaders have choices. Knowing what the options are and which one to use when will help the leader navigate the troubled waters that we call conflict.

MANAGING CONFLICT
with COMPLACENCY

■ I have a colleague, Dr. H. Stanton Tuttle, who is retired from the United States Army. Often we are discussing things occurring around us or problems we are encountering, and he references teaching moments and experiences from his time in the armed services. There always seems to be an example, an anecdote, or application from something that happened in his military career that he can apply to the occasion at hand.

One day while we were talking, he made reference to what he was taught when the service members would be at the firing range. He commented on how individuals would line up and face their targets. The targets were lined up so that every individual firing would have his or her target directly in sight. This was called "your lane." As the troops were about ready to fire their weapons, the officer in charge would yell, "Ladies and gentlemen, watch your lane."[1]

Watching your lane meant being very aware of the target directly in front of you, in your lane, and making sure you were shooting at it. Apparently, it was easy to get confused and shoot at the target next to your lane, hitting it and altering the outcomes for the person beside you. Likewise, if you shot the wrong target, you would miss yours. So the officer in charge would say, "Watch your lane." Pay attention to the target in your lane.

Conflict management is like the firing range in some ways. A leader may figuratively stand at the line and from this position see many lanes. There may be multiple needs, demands, issues, situations, opportunities, personalities, and more, that are visible throughout the organization. A leader has the unique perspective of seeing the broad landscape of reality. The leader knows there may be more than one target and each may be as valid and worthy as the other.

The reality is a leader can only expend energy and time on that which is in his or her lane. This brings the leader to a unique decision point. If there is another issue looming, the leader either switches attention to it or recognizes that the issue is not the main focal point at the present. Both are valid options. Either option can be the right decision depending on the individual situation.

Admittedly, there may be times when the leader needs to switch issues. The other may be significant enough that the leader feels the need to engage in some form of intervention. The problem with this is if the leader is not careful, he or she can end up constantly jumping from one issue to another, doing nothing more than resolving conflict or putting out fires. While this may feel productive at some level, it may not permit the leader to provide proactive leadership to the organization.

I have heard of a few pastors and organizational leaders who have the reputation of being fixers. They move to a church or organization and spend their energies solving problems. They have a reputation for helping organizations that are in trouble and turmoil work through the issues. Many of these leaders have the unique ability of helping organizations in trouble turn around and change their trajectory.

While we need leaders who have the innate ability to be fixers, many of us are more passionate about proactively leading an organization to the next level of greatness. Leading to the next level of greatness involves "watching our lane." Not everything that we see on the horizon is our immediate problem, nor should it be. It may be that in time as we lead organizational and systemic change, we will influence issues and circumstances, but it doesn't mean they consume us now.

Leaders need to watch their lanes. Leaders need to focus on doing what is necessary to competently and accurately hit the target for which they are aiming while ignoring the looming targets that may be on either side of the real target. This takes concentration, commitment, and follow-through. This means the leader doesn't get sidetracked by surrounding activity but stays focused on the target.

In general, this is good leadership advice. In conflict management, this is imperative. By virtue of being the leader, many things are going to land on your desk. People will expect the leader to understand, get involved, fix the problem, straighten someone out, or bring about any number of possible resolutions. Generally speaking, followers feel it is the leader's job to get involved. The truth is, not every situation or issue that is brought to the attention of the leader warrants the leader's time and energy.

The Use of Complacency

One of the choices a leader can make is to choose complacency as a conflict management technique. Complacency, in this context, means choosing not to get involved. Complacency does not mean a leader is so secure or comfortable that he or she does not want to step out of that comfort zone and risk creating waves. It also does not mean the leader doesn't care. It is recognizing that the issue or situation is currently not in the leader's lane.

Complacency is a conscious and intentional decision. The leader considers the circumstances, the reality, the liability, the consequences, and makes a conscious decision not to get involved. It may be because the nature of the situation does not warrant intervention by the organizational leader. It may be because there is limited liability, regardless of the outcome. It may be because the consequences of any outcome are minimal and will not change reality.

The leader who engages in conflicted situations where the outcome will have minimal impact is a leader who is risking a lot to possibly change a little. The question to be answered is, what is really worth engaging in intervention? Someone once said, "Choose carefully what you are willing to shed blood for, because everything is not worth the shedding of blood."

One organizational leader took great care in ensuring the organization for which he was in charge ran smoothly and efficiently. The necessary time was spent preparing, distributing, and discussing an employee handbook that outlined virtually every contractual and implied commitment of the organization and the employee. Employees were provided a revised copy annually and required to sign a form stating they received it and were encouraged to read it. The employee handbook was the official document for employer-employee relations.

One of the benefits this organization gave to its employees was a paid lunch break. It was one way the organization felt it could provide a valued benefit at a relatively low cost. For the most part, employees appreciated the benefit and did not take advantage of it. As long as an employee was sensitive to time and completed the assigned work, lunch breaks were not monitored. Employees were trusted.

Within one department, there was an employee who faithfully came to work and did her job. Over time, the leader learned that this individual was coming to work, eating breakfast at work after her time started, taking two breaks—one in the midmorning and one in the midafternoon, leaving on time, and enjoying the paid lunch break. For the leader it seemed a bit unusual that the person would be eating breakfast at work and enjoying the other paid break times.

The leader decided to inquire from this person's supervisor about her pattern. The supervisor defended the employee, stating she did her work, she did it well, and while she was eating breakfast, she was reading documentation from the previous day for information that would influence the work of that department. The supervisor indicated she did not have any concerns about the situation. The leader, knowing the supervisor, understood that if the supervisor did have a problem, she would certainly address it.

Now, the leader had a choice to make. The employee, on the one hand, appeared to be taking advantage of the employer-employee relationship with the amount of paid break time. On the other hand, the supervisor not only held that the employee was doing her work and doing it well but even justified the breakfast time. The leader was conflicted. Was this employee taking advantage of the organization? Was the situation creating inequity between employees?

The leader elected to do a little more assessment about what really happens throughout the day among employees and the amount of time spent on paid breaks. After an informal review, the leader learned that many of the employees would often have a snack at their desk or workstation and munch while working. Likewise, no one appeared to be taking advantage of the paid break time. In this individual situation, the employee's immediate supervisor was pleased with her work output. The leader decided to leave things alone and not try to force the issue. Essentially, the leader chose complacency as the appropriate response to dealing with this situation.

Complacency is about choosing not to get involved. In the case above, the leader did do some informal assessment and made sure he had all of the facts to help guide the decision-making process. At the end of the day, the leader chose to leave well enough alone and let the supervisor deal with those who directly reported to her as she deemed appropriate. Intervening would have meant undermining the supervisor, micromanaging details, adversely impacting employee morale, and adding more monitoring to ensure everyone complied. The leader made a conscious and intentional decision that considered the circumstances and consequences of intervening. This leader concluded the liability of intervention was not worth the price to be paid.

Complacency Is Not a Cop-Out

Complacency should never be a cop-out for ignoring conflict. *Merriam-Webster* defines the verb "cop out" to mean "to avoid or neglect problems, responsibilities, or commitments."[2] By "cop-out" (the noun), we are talking about "an instance of" or "an excuse for" avoiding situations and circumstances that are potentially conflicted because we do not want to face them.[3]

There was a seasoned pastor who was serving a local church that represented the norm for his faith tradition. The pastor seemingly was taking care of his pastoral duties, and all indicators were that he was loved and respected by most of the people in the church. This pastor made friends with a young pastor who served a nearby church of the same tradition. The two of them begin to socialize together. Not long into their friendship, the younger pastor noticed that the seasoned pastor was doing things and saying things that seemingly contradicted the young pastor's view of pastoral integrity.

The young pastor was not sure what, if anything, he should say or do about his observations. There were several things that concerned the young pastor, but there were a couple of things that the young pastor believed were taboo in their faith tradition. The young pastor finally decided to seek counsel from his supervisory leadership. The young pastor shared his concerns, to which the supervisor replied, "If it is not illegal or immoral, I don't want to know about it."

After assuring the supervisory leader that the incidents were neither illegal nor immoral, the conversation concluded. For the seasoned pastor, the benefit of the doubt was clearly given by the supervisor. No doubt the seasoned pastor's tenure and current success spoke volumes into the situation. For the young pastor, a shadow of doubt was cast on his own understanding of pastoral ministry. To the young pastor's knowledge, nothing was ever said and neither the incidents nor the conversation were ever mentioned again.

This young pastor was new in the ministry and was framing his view of pastoral ministry. While he had not been prepared for situations like this in college and seminary, he wanted to believe in the integrity of the profession. Instead, it felt as though the leadership copped out. No one will ever really know if the supervisor copped out or if the response is the standard by which all things are judged in that tradition. What the young pastor learned was integrity must mean different things for different people or at least in different situations. Today, for different reasons, neither of the pastors is pastoring local churches.

Copping out is a dangerous way to address conflict. Some may describe it as the ostrich approach, which means we hide our head in the sand and pretend it does not exist. Ignoring conflict because we do not want to deal with it is an unhealthy way of handling conflict. We have choices for how we deal with conflict, and complacency is one of them, but it is not a cop-out.

When to Be Complacent

Choosing the technique of complacency can be as difficult as choosing some other technique of conflict management. While it may make sense to the leader who is making the choice, others may see it as the leader acting like an ostrich.

Others may even think the leader is just simply copping out because he or she is afraid to get involved. The question looms, when is complacency the right choice?

A leader must consider the circumstances. Is the situation something that is directly connected to the organization? Is the situation something where the organization or people in the organization will be hurt and to what degree? For a leader to get involved, the situation at hand must directly impact the organization or its people in a way that it will be detrimental if nothing is done. Complacency is a great choice if the direct connection to the organization is missing and no one is directly involved.

To what degree can the leader influence the situation? One of the questions the leader has to ask is whether he or she has the authority to make a difference or whether the situation is within his or her domain of responsibility. Because leaders are viewed as professionals, sometimes people turn to them for assistance. If the situation is beyond a leader's locus of control and he or she does not have the institutional authority to address it, not engaging is the best option.

Managing reality is really about managing the perception of reality. Sometimes conflict is more perception than reality. While both are extremely threatening, a leader needs to be careful not to get caught up in the whirlwind of perception surrounding conflict. It is easy to be caught up in the mania of conflict and never see the real issue at hand. A leader needs to be very careful in sorting out reality and identifying exactly what issue is at hand. Until then, complacency is a great way to combat misguided perception.

Some conflict has the potential to create liability. A leader is responsible to protect the organization and its people from liability exposure. Some would define this as risk management.

Leaders must be in the business of risk management all of the time. When conflict arises, a leader needs to understand the amount of risk to which the organization or its people are exposed. Likewise, the leader needs to know what the liability is of this exposure. This could be financial, legal, physical safety, defamation, or something else. Electing to intervene may be driven by the degree of severity and the liability involved. If there is no liability, complacency may be a reasonable choice in conflict management.

Like liability, the projected consequences of a situation may determine if intervention is necessary. If the conflicted situation has the potential to create severely negative outcomes that will have adverse consequential damage on the organization or its people, then intervention may be appropriate. If the outcomes have little to no projected consequences, not intervening may be a good choice.

For a leader to intervene where he or she does not have to is dangerous territory. It is risky enough to engage when the issue or situation warrants it. Doing it when it is not required does nothing more than cause people to think or say that the leader is just throwing his or her authority around or flexing his or her power muscles.

Complacency is a legitimate response to dealing with conflict. It should never be a cop-out because an individual is too scared or does not have enough of a vested interest to engage. It should be a conscious and intentional choice driven by circumstances, reality, liability, and the potential consequences.

Even Jesus chose complacency, or so it seems, when he encountered the Pharisees who were trying to trip him up:

Then the Pharisees went out and laid plans to trap him [Jesus] in his words. They sent their disciples to him along with the Herodians. "Teacher," they said, "we know that you are a man of integrity and that you teach the way of God in accordance with the truth. You aren't swayed by others, because you pay no attention to who they are. Tell us then, what is your opinion? Is it right to pay the imperial tax to Caesar or not?"

But Jesus, knowing their evil intent, said, "You hypocrites, why are you trying to trap me? Show me the coin used for paying the tax." They brought him a denarius, and he asked them, "Whose image is this? And whose inscription?"

"Caesar's," they replied.

Then he said to them, "So give back to Caesar what is Caesar's, and to God what is God's." (Matt. 22:15-21)

Jesus responded to the Pharisees in Socratic fashion by answering their questions with questions. He wanted them to critically think about what they were trying to do. He also was not going to give them the evidence they were hoping to find. He was not going to implicate himself. He simply chose complacency, using questions to challenge them to consider what they were asking and doing.

In some circumstances, the use of complacency allows a leader to leave the issue resting with the other side. Rather than owning the issue, reacting to the issue, or acting on the issue, the leader using complacency is permitted the choice not to get involved, and the issue remains with the originator.

It is striking that Jesus referred to the intent of the Pharisees as evil. The truth is, sometimes conflict is just plain evil. While it not recommended calling those with whom you are having conflict names (e.g., hypocrites), it is important to recognize the source and intent of the conflict. This requires spiritual maturity and wisdom along with good assessment. As leaders understand the intent and goal of the conflict, they may just discover that it is not worthy of intervention beyond complacency.

The Perils of Not Choosing Complacency

When leaders refuse to use complacency when it would be the most appropriate response, the risks are high. Focused leadership is about knowing where you are going, how you are going to get there, and how you know when you arrive. In the words of the officer in charge, watch your lane. When a leader loses sight of the target because he or she is focusing on another target, that leader will miss the true mark. To say it another way, when a leader is always bouncing from perceived problem to perceived problem, proactive leadership is not likely to happen. It is hard to provide authentic leadership when you are always seeing a problem that needs to be fixed.

The risk of trying to be a fixer is being perceived as someone who is always intervening in everything. This creates a credibility issue for a leader. Can a leader be trusted when that leader is always trying to get involved where he or she may not even be welcome? Is the leader's involvement stunting the growth of the followers to resolve their own issues?

There was a younger pastor who served a good church in a nice community. Not everything was perfect, but it appeared to be a wonderful place to serve. One Sunday evening following a service, the pastor confronted a couple outside the church about something they were doing with which he disagreed. The conversation turned ugly, and the pastor and the family ended up saying things both would regret. Unfortunately, the emotions ran deep and nearly turned the conversation into a physical fight. Finally, the pastor walked away.

The pastor, on the heels of those few moments, made a hasty decision. He decided to quit. He called a confidant who understood pastoral ministry and informed him of his very recent decision. The confidant explored the issue with the pastor. Other than resigning immediately, the pastor did not have a plan. He did not have another church waiting for him, which meant he would be unemployed. He risked being homeless, because his family lived in church-owned housing. The pastor was sure of only one thing: he was done with that church.

The confidant tried to talk the pastor out of this decision, encouraging him to stay at least long enough to find another church. In addition, the confidant reminded the pastor that per church policy, he had to give notice. The pastor refused to accept any kind of advice and within twenty-four hours of that Sunday evening service resigned without notice, never doing another act of pastoral service for that church. He did move and began seeking another ministry opportunity.

That heated Sunday evening conversation changed the course of direction for that pastor and his family. It changed the course of direction for that church. The question that must be asked is, what if that pastor had chosen complacency? If the pastor had simply left things alone, at least for the evening, would things have been different for him, his family, and for the church? We were not there, and we cannot surmise any perfect answer. The good news is everything worked out for the pastor and his family because they eventually moved to another pastorate. The church he left called another pastor and continued ministry to the community.

The retired military friend I identified at the beginning of this chapter often uses the following phrase when we are discussing things happening around us: "It's not my lane." While watching one's lane is critically important, it is equally important to know what is not in one's lane. When something is beyond a leader's area of expertise, control, authority, or responsibility, or when the timing is just not right, complacency is a valid option. Complacency can help keep a leader from being sidetracked by all the surrounding activity. Knowing when to intervene is learning to perfect the idea of watching your lane. When it is not your lane, complacency is a good choice.

MANAGING CONFLICT
with CONFRONTATION

■ It was Sunday following the evening service. The pastor's day had been intense. It began with getting up early to review the sermon for Sunday morning, followed by Sunday school, the morning worship service, dinner with guests, spending a few minutes with family in the afternoon, excusing himself to review Sunday evening's Bible study, and then leading the evening Bible study. No doubt the pastor was drained, if not exhausted. After most of the good-byes were given, the pastor went out the door to head for home. He was looking forward to some quiet time and a good night's rest.

The pastor was less than twenty feet from the church door when one of the faithful members confronted him. It was obvious by the tone and body language that this parishioner was upset. For what seemed like an hour but was probably just a few minutes, the church member told the pastor what was wrong, what he could do to "fix" it, and when he should do it. Without leaving any detail to the imagination, the church member had agitatedly articulated the issue at hand.

The pastor was not prepared for this conversation. Not only was he not prepared, but also he was physically and mentally spent and in no frame of mind to be dealing with it then. In the heat of the moment the pastor responded to the faithful member, "I appreciate you being concerned and bringing this to my attention; however, Sunday night is not the best time to do this. Why don't you wait, call tomorrow when you are not so *carnal*, and arrange a meeting for us to discuss it."

The moment the pastor said this, he felt bad. In many ways he spoke the truth (and without a doubt in love), but did he really just call one of the faithful church members *carnal?* Was the confrontational attack of the member worthy of the pastor's own confrontational response? Could the pastor redeem this or did he just excommunicate a full-fledged, tithe-paying church member?

The Use of Confrontation

When we think of confrontation, we think of words such as "in your face" or "let's get it on." Typically, we think of an aggressive type of behavior with which we are confronting another person. The dictionary defines confrontation as the "clashing of forces or ideas."[1] Generally speaking, confrontation is at least two opposing perspectives coming face-to-face, meeting each other on opposite sides. It may feel like a battle and at times like a war. Battles and wars are fought to be won. Going into conflict from a confrontational stance incites emotions and thoughts about the projected outcome. I have known a few people who like to argue just for the sake of arguing, but most of the time if something is worth the confrontation, the plan is to "win." Consequently, emotions are engaged and thought processes are rapid. We feel and think things in the moment that we would generally not feel or think. But this is confrontation, and we will do whatever is necessary to make sure we come out the victor. It is the natural tendency of human nature.

Consequently, the confrontational stance calls on our defense mechanisms. We have a plan, position, reputation, idea, or vision to protect. Since it is ours, we are going to do everything within our power to preserve what we believe is worth protecting. Confrontation can easily become personal, biased, one sided, and irrational.

For the most part, faith leaders take a dim view of confrontation. Everything we understand about faith, love, and a Christlike spirit challenges us to avoid direct confrontation. We see little to no value in wars or battles. Preserving a Christian testimony is more important than winning at any cost. Because we know how emotion and irrational thought processes creep into confrontation, we try to keep interactions stable and logical. Confrontation just isn't part of a Christian response to conflict, or is it?

One of the best referenced examples of confrontation is found in the Synoptic Gospels: "Jesus entered the temple area and drove out all who were buying and selling there. He overturned the tables of the money changers and the benches of those selling doves. 'It is written,' he said to them, "'My house will be called a house of prayer,'" but you are making it "a den of robbers'"'" (Matt. 21:12-13).

The Scriptures give this account of Jesus entering the temple area to find the place desecrated. While buying and selling were acceptable for the purposes of purchasing approved sacrifices, Jesus found the intentions of those involved less than holy. They had ignored the purpose, function, and sanctity of the temple to make it a common marketplace and for some a perfunctory act of worship. Jesus, on seeing this, confronted the people, proclaimed truth, identified wrong, and cast the ill-intended out of the temple area. Confrontational?

When Jesus confronted the buyers and sellers, there were three dynamics in play: (1) There was the desecration of the temple. The house of worship was not meant to be a common marketplace. (2) There were the misaligned priorities of the people. The temple was to be a place of prayer and worship. (3) There was the authority of Jesus. Jesus was the representation of God on earth—he was the true Temple, God dwelling among his people—and authority had been invested in him to carry out his Father's work.

Are there times when the use of confrontation is appropriate as a faith leader? This depends on the individual dynamics of the situation. Hopefully, there are other options, choices leaders can make that will be less "in your face." On the other hand, there may be times when confrontation is the best option. While confrontation should not be the default approach for addressing conflict, it is very possible that there are times when it is the most appropriate.

A young pastor in a suburban church was working very hard to build the church. God was honoring the work of all the people. The church was growing, new people were attending, and people's lives were being changed. One of the new attendees was a young man who was recently married. After a few months, people started commenting to the pastor about how this young man was always hanging around the children and youth, especially the girls. While no inappropriate activity was known to have happened, people's "flags" were being raised to a behavior that was atypical for an adult male in the church.

One day, one of the parishioners told the pastor about an incident in which this young man was seen with one of the teens of the church exhibiting behavior that was inappropriate for an adult with a minor; however, it was not illegal at this point. The pastor felt it was time for intervention. Choosing confrontation, the pastor invited the young man to a meal at a local restaurant. The pastor explained the concern, confronting the young man about his behavior and intent. The pastor was extremely emphatic and in no uncertain terms informed the young man that any future activity or behavior that was deemed inappropriate would be reported to the authorities. The young man acknowledged he understood, and the two departed.

The young man continued to come to church with his bride but failed to settle into the fold. Fortunately, his behavior toward the children and youth improved, but that could be because other adults in the church were watching with keen eyes. Likewise, he was closely supervised when engaged in activities where there could be any hint of improper conduct. The result was limited opportunity for him to be inappropriate.

The pastor could have chosen to handle this situation in a variety of ways; however, he chose confrontation. The dynamic of the situation warranted it. This young man was behaving in ways that contradicted appropriate behavior for those in the church and compromised the safety and well-being of others in the church. Addressing the conflict head on seemed to be the best choice for this situation.

Far too often the line of conflict is fuzzy, and ascertaining the facts is difficult. In a few and much more rare occasions, the line is much clearer. When the line of conflict is clear and the situation falls outside the limits of scriptural precept and principle, it is much easier to consider confrontation as an option for dealing with conflict.

Again, using the example of the temple, the motives, attitudes, and activities of the buyers and sellers were misaligned. Rather than seeking God, some were seeking to simply fulfill their duty and others to profit from the circumstances. Sometimes people join great organizations, not for how they can contribute and make them better, but for what they can get out of them. Occasionally, an individual can sow seeds of distraction, discontent, and discord to the degree it hinders an organization. When this happens, something must be done.

There was a small church of really close young couples. They were like one big happy family. One day, one of the young men was distraught. He learned his wife, and mother of their children, had participated in an extramarital affair. The couple ended up divorcing. Others in the church began to look for answers and arrived at the conclusion that if the pastor would have done his "job," this would not have happened. Needless to say, things went from bad to worse for the pastor and the church.

The pastor who was graciously trying to deal with this situation was seemingly having his character assassinated. In an attempt to clear the air, the pastor confronted one of the young couples who seemed to be the source of the distraction and discord. Unfortunately, the conversation did not go well, and the character assassination continued. It was not long before the pastor resigned and moved to another ministry opportunity.

Confrontation is a risky conflict management technique. There are times when it is appropriate and necessary. Sometimes confronting a person directly is the best way to address the situation and look for a way to manage or resolve the conflict. On the other hand, it always comes with risk; something could potentially be misinterpreted, misstated, or misused, and the situation grow bleaker. Even with the best of intentions, confrontation can lead to more confrontation.

Choosing confrontation as a conflict management technique is appropriate when the situation is so severe that something must be done. When the danger is imminent, the potential fallout is massive, the liability is too large a risk, or people's lives are at stake, addressing the conflict head on may be the best option.

To choose confrontation as a management tool for conflict assumes that the person doing the confronting has a vested interest, if not the authority, to engage at this level. All of us have met people who like confrontational settings. These folks, once they are found out, are often dismissed for not having a vested interest but just liking the "fight." To use confrontation effectively, one must demonstrate a passion for the cause and have a vested interest in the outcome.

For faith leaders, the passion and interest is often twofold: (1) leaders have a responsibility for the organizations they are charged to lead, and (2) leaders have an inherent authority to engage in the conflicted situation. Jesus was the true Temple and as such had the authority and power to rebuke and remove those who were desecrating the temple area.

Confrontation is often an expression of authority or power. When a leader chooses to use confrontation, he or she is exercising "power" in an attempt to control a situation, manage people, or resolve conflict. A leader can and must do this when necessary; however, it is not the default mechanism for dealing with every situation. It should be used sparingly as deemed appropriate and when other options may not be as effective.

It is important for a leader to understand that choosing confrontation as a conflict management technique clearly places the leader on one side of the issue. It is very difficult, if not impossible, to choose confrontation as a conflict management technique and not articulate or demonstrate on which side of the issue the leader is standing. The inherent risk is separating oneself from those who are on the opposite side or being labeled with a stance on a position or situation. A wise leader will consider the risk involved before choosing to use confrontation to intervene in conflict.

In the example at the beginning of this chapter, once the word "carnal" flew out of the pastor's mouth that Sunday evening after church, the faithful parishioner recognized the conversation would need to happen at another time. The two bid each other a good night and went their separate ways. Who really knows what the parishioner was thinking. Did his pastor really call him *carnal?* The pastor later reported feeling terrible about the confrontation. He couldn't believe that he was so reactive and blurted out what he was feeling with such boldness. Could anything be said or done that would redeem the relationship and bring restoration?

The good news is that later in the week, the two did meet and discuss the issue that seemed so urgent on Sunday evening. Ironically, it didn't seem to be so urgent, but it was important. Both identified emotion and exhaustion as being culprits of their respective behaviors. The faithful parishioner humorously acknowledged his bad timing and "carnal spirit." The pastor apologized, listened to the concerns, and began to work toward resolving the issue.

Confrontation Is an Intentional Choice

Confrontation can occur anytime, anywhere, and in a myriad of ways. Being drawn into conflict as the pastor was on Sunday evening is not an appropriate way of managing conflict. All leaders are susceptible to this trap when others come to them with issues, concerns, situations, perceived problems, complaints, and more. While the point of the confrontation may be real and important, this is not the time to choose confrontation in return. The wise leader understands confrontation, not as the conflict, but as a conflict management technique to use when it is absolutely necessary.

Doing a threat assessment and considering the risk is an important component of choosing confrontation. The pastor, who felt his character was being assassinated, after the couple divorced, chose confrontation. In the end, the risk was too great. The relationships and trust embedded in the fellowship of believers in that church was strong. Trying to rationalize, objectify, and alter the perception was too difficult. The unfortunate set of circumstances led to the pastor's tenure at the church being shortened.

Choosing confrontation when principles, precepts, or people are at risk is an appropriate intervention. The pastor who confronted the young man hanging out with the children and youth knew there was a lot at stake. The pastor had the responsibility to protect the flock. As pastor, he had the inherent authority to intervene. Not every situation or conflicted issue falls into this arena, but when it does, confrontation may be the right choice.

It is essentially impossible to take a position or stance on an issue to the degree of confrontation and not come down clearly on one side. At this point, the wise leader considers all of the information available and makes the best-informed choice. Reacting from feelings and raw emotion will only get the leader in trouble. Likewise, reacting based on prior incidents is a sure recipe for disaster. Leaders must make informed decisions and confront only when it is the right choice.

Leaders should never back away from a conflicted situation because they are afraid to intervene. Just as the wise leader does not go looking for conflict, he or she also knows when a conflicted situation warrants intervention through confrontation. These occurrences are probably few and far between but cannot be ignored just because the leader does not want to get involved. Sometimes the best choice is confrontation.

Confrontation is a matter of intentionality. Using confrontation as a conflict management technique is a matter of being intentional in the response to conflict. Not all conflict will demand or warrant a confrontational approach. Leaders must be able to assess situations and determine what the best approach is. When confrontation appears to be the right choice, a leader must respond accordingly.

Leaders should not feel unspiritual when they elect to use confrontation. Because confrontation is defined as a head-on encounter with a negative connotation, it feels evil or non-Christlike. The truth is, confronting someone for the right reason may very well be the most Christlike thing that can be done in a situation. This is not to say a leader should be callous and press ahead regardless. It is to say that when the situation calls for confrontation, a leader should be poised and prepared to move into action. It is an intentional choice.

A midlevel leader in a large organization was dealing with a situation that seemingly was not improving. This leader had several individuals directly reporting to him. One of those individuals was not performing at a level that met the organization's expectations or furthered the goals of the division to which this person was assigned. The leader tried several techniques to motivate, lead, guide, and direct this individual but to no avail.

During a formal review process, the leader identified, in tandem with the person in question, a specific plan of action for the next review period. Both felt the expectations were reasonable and agreed that they were realistic. The leader's perception was that this person would be focused and able to attack the specific plan of action.

During the next review process, the leader and this person reviewed the specific plan of action that had been developed in their last formal meeting. Much to the dismay of the leader, very little progress had been made toward the goals. The division's benchmarks were missed in those areas where this individual was responsible. The person offered excuses, cast blame, and promised to improve.

The leader was faced with a difficult choice: allow the trend to continue or confront the issue head on. The leader chose to confront the issue, being very intentional to lean on the facts of the situation. It was a difficult conversation as the leader identified the work that was not completed, explained that the division had not met its benchmarks as a result, and spelled out the long-term ramifications for the organization. The leader recognized that it was his responsibility to own this as the supervisor. By virtue of his position, he had the authority to address it. Ultimately, the leader made it very clear where the person in question stood and what the plan of action was going to be. Since this issue had lagged over time and continued to be an issue, the leader elected to discharge the individual.

In this case, the leader chose confrontation as an intentional response to addressing the issue at hand. He was responsible and accountable for the work of the division. He had the authority to address the situation. It was risky. It clearly defined his position. The leader did not cowardly back away but stood tall and led using confrontation to manage a difficult situation.

One of the intentional choices faith leaders can make is to use confrontation when it is necessary. As previously stated, it is not a default reaction but an intentional decision to address a conflicted situation. Confrontation does not mean leaders compromise their faith or integrity. It means they are courageous enough to own responsibility for the situation and to exercise enough authority to create positive change.

MANAGING CONFLICT
with COMMUNICATION

■ A faith-based human-service agency had been discussing the need for new chairs in its waiting area. The current chairs were old, well used, and took up significant floor space because of their size. Although the chairs were functional and in reasonable shape for their age, the consensus was they needed to be replaced if for no other reason than to free up space and make things look less congested.

One day, one of the program directors for the agency volunteered to do some comparison shopping and see if she could find nice chairs that would work in a public waiting area and at a good price. She understood there was a balance between quality and what the agency could justify spending on the chairs, especially since the agency had chairs that served the need. After a couple of weeks of looking around, she presented a proposal to the executive director that they purchase the chairs at a local office-supply business. The chairs were average business quality, a nice size, and at a price the agency could justify. The agency director gave her his blessing to proceed with the purchase.

A week or so later, the chairs were delivered to the agency. The old ones were carted off; the new ones placed. Everything seemed to have worked out fine until another program director saw the chairs. On seeing the chairs, she immediately went to the executive director's office and inquired. The executive director explained how the process went and that he authorized the purchase. While the program director understood, she was not pleased with the decision.

Over the next couple of days, the executive director learned the two program directors were discussing the change. The one who took the initiative, did the shopping, and made the purchase felt good about the change and believed it was a positive step for the agency. The one who was not pleased could not believe that such a decision was made. Their conversations turned into conflict.

The program director that made the purchase felt her ability to make good decisions was being questioned. As others became aware of the conflict, this program director felt that others were looking down on her. She felt she was being personally attacked. The situation negatively impacted her happiness in the workplace, compromised her relationships with a few others, and made her feel less than competent to do the job she was hired to do and did well.

This program director came to the executive director and informed him that she could not work under such scrutiny. She expressed her concerns, identified the feelings with which she was wrestling, and essentially threw her hands up in resignation of doing anything except her specific job.

The executive director knew it was time to intervene. He requested a meeting with the two program directors. At the appointed time, the three of them met to explore how this situation turned into the present conflict between them and the impact it was having on others who worked or volunteered at the agency.

The executive director began by recounting the facts as they occurred. He described how there were discussions about replacing the chairs and how the process progressed to making that happen. He also owned the fact that he approved the purchase. Once he laid the foundation, he asked the program directors to elaborate on what they were thinking and feeling.

The program director who made the purchase laid out her concerns and feelings. She explained that she was trying to do something good for the agency, spent time away from her regular work to make it happen, and now felt ostracized by others. She talked about how the conflict was impacting her performance at work. She shared that she felt the other program director was questioning her ability and discrediting her.

Once that program director was finished, the other program director began with her side of the story. She started with an apology and a sincere acknowledgment that she was not trying to discredit the first program director, make her look incompetent, or negatively impact her. She agreed that the decision to purchase new chairs was good. She acknowledged that the price seemed right and demonstrated good stewardship of agency resources. She liked that they took up less room in the waiting area.

Both the program director who made the purchase and the executive director were a little perplexed. If the unhappy program director felt that way about the decision, then why did this turn into conflict? Was it because she was not consulted ahead of time? Did she have a better plan that had not been shared? What was the real issue?

The executive director trying to mediate the conflict asked the unhappy program director why she was not pleased with the chairs. After all, if she liked the decision, the price, and the extra space and did not have to do the work to make it happen, what was the issue? The program director stated her concern: the chairs were cloth instead of vinyl.

After comprehending what this program director was saying, the executive director asked for more clarification. The program director explained. She had worked at the agency for many years. Her office was in the proximity of the waiting area. Over the years, she had seen many spills, messes, crayon marks, ink, and more, on the chairs. Either she or someone else would have to clean them up. Because the old chairs were vinyl, they were easier to clean. With the new chairs being cloth, they will not clean up as easily, and over time they will show more stains and wear and thus need to be replaced sooner.

The executive director was almost flabbergasted. Her answer was so practical, so realistic, and so reasonable. Her passion about the present and the future of what the agency did was so obvious. She was concerned that the right decision be made now to guard the future. She was not upset, disappointed with the initiative of the other program director, or crazy. She was simply looking at the situation through a lens in which neither the other program director nor the executive director were looking.

After talking this through, the decision was made to return the chairs, since the agency had the option, and purchase new chairs, the same type of chairs but with vinyl covering. Within a few days the agency had new chairs in the waiting area that looked great, took up less floor space, and were vinyl. More importantly, the present conflict was resolved.

The Use of Communication

Communication as a conflict management technique resembles the familiar process of conflict management known as mediation. Mediation is the "intervention between conflicting parties to promote reconciliation, settlement, or compromise."[1] When individuals or groups are in the midst of conflict and cannot arrive at a resolution, they may turn to an independent, nonbiased third party to guide the process.

Faith leaders are frequently called on to be mediators. People look to their leadership, in the context of faith, to manage controversy, disagreements, differences of perspectives, and diverse opinions. It is not uncommon for a leader to be asked to mediate between two individuals or groups of individuals simply because of his or her role as a leader. When called on, a leader is expected to be the expert and have the ability to bring about resolution.

A single mother was struggling financially to make ends meet for her teenage son and herself. She lived on the edge of poverty and probably only survived by living in public housing, where the rent was subsidized. Once her son graduated from high school and got a job, she expected that he would contribute a portion of his income to the household. The son protested, believing that it was not his responsibility even though he still lived in the apartment.

As a desperate measure, the mother invited their pastor over to mediate a conversation between her and her son on the issue of the son assisting financially. The mother was anticipating the clergy siding with her. The son was blindsided. The clergy, who may not have even known why he was asked to visit, was expected to be the voice of authority to illuminate truth in this matter.

Leaders will become involved in all kinds of conflicted circumstances. Some are critical and may impact the whole organization. Some are less critical but important to those involved. Some will be so confidential that they will seem like covert operations. Whatever the situation, leaders are assumed to be knowledgeable and capable of resolving such conflicts.

This is where communication comes into the leader's tool kit. Using any of the techniques of mediation, such as active listening, "I" messages, and reframing, the leader mediating the conflict will attempt to open the lines of communication between the conflicting parties. He or she will try to create an open and honest dialogue where people are being heard, the root causes of the conflict are exposed, and the resolution becomes apparent.

In the Gospels is an account of James and John coming to Jesus and making a special request: "Then James and John, the sons of Zebedee, came to him. 'Teacher,' they said, 'we want you to do for us whatever we ask.' 'What do you want me to do for you?' he asked. They replied, 'Let one of us sit at your right and the other at your left in your glory'" (Mark 10:35-37).

Apparently, James and John felt they deserved to flank Jesus when they all entered his kingdom. This would give the two of them position and prestige. In this role, they probably assumed they would be served by those under them. According to Matthew's gospel, their mother may have put them up to this or even asked the favor of Jesus herself (see 20:20). Either way, this didn't go over well with the other ten apostles: "When the ten heard about this, they became indignant with James and John" (Mark 10:41).

This incident prompted Jesus to move into conflict management mode to address the issue:

> Jesus called them together and said, "You know that those who are regarded as rulers of the Gentiles lord it over them, and their high officials exercise authority over them. Not so with you. Instead, whoever wants to become great among you must be your servant, and whoever wants to be first must be slave of all. For even the Son of Man did not come to be served, but to serve, and to give his life as a ransom for many. (Vv. 42-45)

Jesus took this incident and turned it into a teaching moment. With all twelve of the apostles gathered together, he outlined what was problematic with the request that had been made of him. His immediate response to James and John was to inform them that it was not up to him to grant seats of honor but that "these places" belonged "to those for whom they have been prepared" (v. 40). Then he turned his teaching to helping all of them understand what it means to be a true servant leader.

Jesus identified three principles that the apostles needed to consider: (1) that servant leadership is not about lording it over others, (2) that servant leadership is not about exercising authority, and (3) that servant leadership is about serving others. These principles became the foundation for him to work through the issue at hand.

Jesus' intent in identifying this issue and expounding on it was to bring the Twelve back to center. He wanted them to keep their focus. He wanted them to remember who they were, why they were called, and how they should conduct themselves. Even though he turned this conversation into a teaching moment, he was establishing a level playing field where all twelve of the apostles would know that there were no favorites or promises of prestige. Further, he wanted them to understand what it means to lead by serving.

One may surmise that Jesus had two goals in this moment: (1) to ensure James and John understood the seriousness of the self-seeking behavior they were exhibiting and (2) to eliminate the indignation the other apostles felt toward James and John. Jesus used the moment to communicate truth and principle in order to help the apostles recapture the heart of servant leadership.

Principles of Communication

The principles Jesus was teaching in this situation are relevant for using communication as a conflict management technique. The whole issue with James and John revolved around feelings of superiority or feelings that they were deserving of special treatment. There appears to be a feeling of entitlement held by the two apostles or their mother.

Conflict often arises when someone or a group of people believe that they deserve something a certain way, that a specific thing should happen, or that their opinion should be validated. There may be multiple reasons, but those who are at the

MANAGING CONFLICT with COMMUNICATION

heart of an issue may, without acknowledging it, have a sense of entitlement that their perspective is the right one. It is like the sentiment of a humorous plaque: "There are two ways of doing things: my way and the wrong way."

People at the heart of conflict may be strongly opinionated, biased, or simply working from incomplete information. Whatever the foundation of their perspective, they believe that their perspective is right. When others encounter this and disagree, conflict can occur. The result is two sides of some issue.

Faith leaders may want to use communication to help people talk through the feelings and perceived reality that their opinion is the right opinion. Jesus did this in the context of drawing an analogy to servant leadership. Faith certainly gives faith leaders a platform to apply biblical principles and lead people through the framing of perspectives in a Christian context.

Communication also balances power in conflict. Jesus talked about the misuse of authority and how those in charge exercised authority over others. Conflict may arise from situations where those with the perceived power are holding it over those who may not have power. No doubt, organizations are built with a distribution of power; however, a biblical principle would be that those with the power not use it as a tool to control others. Again, Jesus was drawing his listeners' minds to what it means to serve others.

Communication may include helping those in conflict assume responsibility for their opinions and judgments. This is done in a nonthreatening and exploratory way; however, it is extremely important for getting to the root cause of the conflict. James and John needed to understand the behavior they were exhibiting. Once people assume ownership of their feelings and perspectives, they can move toward resolution much easier.

89

As a leader helps sort out responsibility, hopefully both sides will see the facts as they really are and not how they appeared. Communication can help reframe situations, circumstances, issues, feelings, and reality so that everyone can see the true picture. In so doing, the root cause of the problem is exposed. When this happens in an authentic and sincere manner, people are more likely to assume ownership for their part of the conflict.

Inherent in all of us is some kind of problem-solving skill or coping mechanism. For some, it is healthy, and for others, it is less so. There are those whose primal response is to fight. There are others who will run. One challenge for the leader using communication is helping those involved identify ways of managing or coping with the conflict. Finding a resolution is the optimal solution. In some cases, people will need guidance and help in knowing how to handle it, maybe how to feel, and certainly how to respond to others who are involved.

Communication is about bringing both sides together. It is about minimizing, and hopefully resolving, conflicted situations. It is about helping conflicted parties sort through the truths. It is about both parties moving past feelings of indignation to brotherly love.

A large metropolitan area had several faith-based, not-for-profit organizations serving the area. Each of the organizations did similar programming, so they divided the community up into neighborhoods, and each was responsible for an area. Along the way, the organizations' leaders got together and decided to start a coalition. As a coalition, the leaders would meet together, discuss the challenges and opportunities they were facing, try to partner together on projects, and pray for each other. Every indicator was that this coalition was a successful support to each of the organizations.

Somewhere along the way the coalition had a difference of opinion. Some of the leaders felt strongly about a particular situation, and almost half felt the other way. Their conversations and planning became so contentious that they split. A group of organizations decided that if they could not have things the way they believed were right, they would pull out and start their own coalition. And that is exactly what they did.

After a few years and as leadership changed, the question started being asked, "Why are there two coalitions?" Why couldn't two faith-based coalitions sort out and work through their differences? The leadership acknowledged that if they work through this and become one coalition again, they may be able to accomplish more than if they remain separate.

The leaders decided to involve a professional mediator to help them sort out their differences. For a couple of years, they met together regularly with the mediator. Both sides identified the issues from their perspectives. Both relinquished any right of entitlement or superiority. Both listened to the other side. Finally, they worked through their issues. The newer coalition rejoined the original coalition, and they were once again one group.

It was the act of communicating that permitted the two faith-based coalitions to work through their disagreement and resolve the conflict. In this case, it took a professional mediator to lead that process. By eventually identifying the primary issues, everyone was able to look at the situation objectively. By leaving power, authority, and the sense of entitlement on the table, they were able to open up and find a resolution on which all of them could agree.

Faith leaders are often called on to be mediators in conflicted situations. Occasionally, the faith leader will see the need for a mediator and volunteer to perform that role. At other times, the faith leader may recommend a professional mediator and assist with the arrangements in full support of the process. Either way, the leader is bringing individuals or groups together to talk through the issue.

Using communication, leaders are helping reframe reality. They are guiding the conversation to discover the root cause of the conflict, minimize power and authority, create a context founded on biblical principles, identify real and reasonable resolutions, and help people understand how to respond to the chosen resolution. Communication is one effective way a leader can attempt to manage conflict within his or her sphere of influence.

MANAGING CONFLICT
with COORDINATION

■ A large not-for-profit agency was beginning to struggle with the way the community and especially stakeholders perceived it. People were starting to ask pointed questions about the efficiency of the organization. Board members were becoming less enthusiastic about serving on the board, and a few even quit. The consumers who the organization served were feeling slighted. The financial reports were not reflecting the sustainable growth and measurable outcomes anticipated.

The board members were having trouble wrapping their minds around what was happening. It was true that the nation had been through a major recession and that the landscape of what this organization did was adversely affected. At the same time, the organization had hired a new executive director who was energetic, was creative, and had a strong work ethic. New board members were recruited who brought expertise in management and leadership. Reports provided at meetings were positive and upbeat. The organization continued to fulfill its mission.

There seemed to be a connection missing between what those within the organization and what those without the organization were hearing and believing. From the inside, things were reported to be going well. Any inconsistencies or discrepancies were explained away with what sounded like rational answers. From the outside, it was different. People were skeptical, losing trust, and questioning the integrity of the organization. This was indirectly a reflection on the board of directors and the organization's leadership.

After several months of trying to sort this out, a small task committee was formed to pursue it further. This committee spent hours and hours over a period of a few months searching and digging into every detail of the organization. The committee solicited stakeholder and consumer input, combed through the financials, and evaluated every major change that had been made since this issue started. What the committee did was a great example of an organization doing a thorough assessment that included the history, environment, and culture.

As this committee started winding down its work, the issue was becoming clear. Almost every symptom plaguing the organization pointed back to the way the financials were tracked and what was reported. The irony was that the organization had multiple layers of controls in place to ensure the financials were handled appropriately, accurately, and with accountability. Even with the best controls, it was obvious the financials were not being managed in a way that provided transparency.

Within a few more weeks the committee gave its report to the board. The good news was that there was no hint of embezzlement or intentional misappropriation. The bad news was that things were worse than the board of directors originally thought. While intentional misappropriation was ruled out, there was a major concern about the way the monies were accounted for and how things were reported. It was obvious from the committee's report that two things had to happen immediately: (1) intervention was needed to correct the financial stability of the organization, and (2) change was needed in financial management, reporting, and controls.

The organization's structure was such that the executive director was primarily in charge of ensuring that the processes and controls of financial management were handled accurately and appropriately. While the executive director was well liked and everyone agreed he worked very hard to ensure the success of the organization, the committee also felt it was time to have a crucial discussion with the executive director about the issue at hand.

The sad part of this scenario is that by the time the committee arrived at its conclusions and was beginning to move toward a resolution, many others within and without the organization had lost confidence in it and especially its leadership. Several were calling for new leadership. Board members who had remained faithful to date were threatening to resign. The organization was starting to implode.

The committee, who up to that time had worked quietly and confidentially, had to decide how it was going to handle the resolution. As a matter of integrity and protocol, a report was given to the officers of the board. A decision was made not to bring the matter to the whole board immediately but to meet with the executive director and discuss the concerns. The committee believed the fewer people involved in the details, the greater the probability that the reputation and integrity of the agency could be preserved.

In an effort to diffuse the potential conflict, it was decided that one person from the committee would meet with the executive director and share the concerns of the whole. This meeting would be nonthreatening, informational, and to some extent exploratory. At the appointed time, the two met and the committee representative laid out the findings and concerns. The executive director was not surprised, since he, too, had heard the internal and external rumblings.

The meeting progressed with open communication. It was obvious the executive director was concerned about the agency and its future. He acknowledged the "vote of no confidence" seemingly being touted about his leadership, and he expressed deep concern. After exploring all of the options, he elected to resign to better serve the agency and preserve the reputations of the agency and himself. The two discussed the logistics of that decision and departed on good terms with a plan of action. No doubt this was a difficult decision for all involved.

The Use of Coordination

The scenario above describes how managing conflict with coordination works. It is the idea of attempting to orchestrate the outcome with intentional conversations and movements. It is about planning, scheduling, or organizing activities and events to address concerns and arrive at a resolution that minimizes the conflict at hand.

In many circumstances, there will be a desired outcome, and the conversations and movements by leadership will seek a specific resolution. Essentially, leadership knows or believes that something specific must happen and works to manage logistics for arriving at the desired outcome. It is a matter of getting those with a vested interest together, at a time that is conducive, to discuss the real issue at hand and to make a healthy decision so that the best resolution may be found. Like a conductor leading a symphony, the leader directs the activities and events in managing the conflict to arrive at the desired outcome.

There may be other times when coordination is used to manage the conflicted situation; however, the outcome has more to do with managing the aftermath or consequences than the actual situation itself. For some conflicts the actual result will have minimal impact, but the perception of the decision made could have a profound impact on the organization or someone in it. Leaders may choose coordination in an attempt to protect people or the organization.

Coordination may be both overt and covert. Ethical leaders believe in transparency, and being overt helps the leader feel transparent. Being overt helps keep the leader from feeling he or she is being sneaky and working behind people's backs to make things happen. On the other hand, sometimes leaders may need to be covert in logistical planning just to minimize the potential for fallout before the resolution can occur. Either way, the leader should never compromise integrity to arrive at a desired outcome.

The use of coordination by the leader leaves little doubt where the leader stands on the issue at hand. Every action and step should be calculated with precision. This indicates the leader is moving toward a specific resolution. A leader who chooses coordination as a conflict management technique will clearly define his or her own position and view about the conflict.

One leader was trying to implement an initiative for which he needed buy-in from several other leaders. Each of them was saying he or she was interested but was waiting for confirmation about the others before committing. The leader was getting exhausted going between parties, meeting to meeting, arranging details, only to keep getting stalled at implementation. The leader finally decided to use coordination to arrange an event and conversation where everyone would commit and a decision to move forward could be made.

The leader had a plan. He would invite the leaders in question to a lunch meeting at the same time and location without telling any of them that the others were coming. He thought if he could get all of them together at one time, he could get the commitment he needed and the project could move forward. This was a covert operation, and it did feel a little manipulative; however, it did not compromise integrity. The leader actually hoped the individuals involved would find it humorous. The leader was simply planning to orchestrate events to accomplish what he believed needed to be accomplished. As fate would have it, before he got the lunch scheduled, everyone committed to the initiative.

In the gospel of John, the story is recounted about a woman caught in adultery and how the teachers of the law and the Pharisees attempted to address it with Jesus. The result was Jesus using coordination to manage the conflict:

> But Jesus went to the Mount of Olives. At dawn he appeared again in the temple courts, where all the people

gathered around him, and he sat down to teach them. The teachers of the law and the Pharisees brought in a woman caught in adultery. They made her stand before the group and said to Jesus, "Teacher, this woman was caught in the act of adultery. In the Law Moses commanded us to stone such women. Now what do you say?" They were using this question as a trap, in order to have a basis for accusing him.

But Jesus bent down and started to write on the ground with his finger. When they kept on questioning him, he straightened up and said to them, "Let any one of you who is without sin be the first to throw a stone at her." Again he stooped down and wrote on the ground.

At this, those who heard began to go away one at a time, the older ones first, until only Jesus was left, with the woman still standing there. Jesus straightened up and asked her, "Woman, where are they? Has no one condemned you?"

"No one, sir," she said.

"Then neither do I condemn you," Jesus declared. "Go now and leave your life of sin." (John 8:1-11)

When the teachers of the law and the Pharisees brought this woman to Jesus, they thought they had an ironclad case to trap Jesus. They knew the law was clear that this woman should be stoned. If Jesus would say anything in favor of or against this law, they would find a way to use it against him. It seemed like a solid way to collect evidence against Jesus.

Jesus, knowing their hearts and intent, elected to respond to them in another manner. Instead of answering their question directly, he commanded the situation and started orchestrating the right resolution. He bent down and started writing on the ground. The teachers of the law and the Pharisees kept pressing the question. Jesus straightened up and challenged them with a statement: "Let any one of you who is without sin be the first to throw a stone at her" (v. 7).

If the teachers of the law and the Pharisees were going to use the law as the measure for determining life or death for this woman, Jesus would challenge them to evaluate their own lives in the context of the law. Had they sinned? What did the law say about their sin and due punishment? Could they with a clear conscience stone her while knowing that their own lives fell short of the law of God? One by one, beginning with the oldest, they went away. Keep in mind the conflict at hand was more about trapping Jesus than dealing with the woman who was caught in adultery.

By the end of the event, only Jesus and the woman remained. Jesus used the moment to express love not condemnation. He also commanded her to go and leave her life of sin. He did not tell her what she was doing was not sin, nor did he glaze over it. He was pointed in identifying the issue but did so in the context of demonstrating grace.

Coordination as a conflict management technique is about using conversations, activities, and events to orchestrate a desirable outcome. Jesus could have responded one way or another to the Pharisees and ended up giving them ammunition for their vendetta. Instead, he captured the incident and managed the conversation. His accusers left, and he was able to demonstrate compassion for an adulteress while challenging her to leave her life of sin.

Truths about Coordination

Coordination as a conflict management technique is intentional. It is not something that happens by default. Likewise, it is not something a leader turns to when other types of conflict management styles have failed. People can see right through this. Coordination is a choice made to orchestrate desired outcomes. Once a leader assesses the conflict, he or she chooses coordination as a way to manage the conflict while seeking specific results.

The use of coordination may help a leader deflect direct confrontation and take control of the conflicted situation. Jesus used coordination rather than confronting the teachers of the law and the Pharisees. A leader may know conflict is in the offing. Rather than confronting the issue directly, the leader may choose coordination to arrange activities and events to address the conflict in a manner that is most appropriate and with precise timing.

To the degree it is possible, it is always best to coordinate how one is going to deal with conflict. When leaders rush in, react, or respond instantaneously, the risk increases that the conflict will not be managed or resolved in the best manner possible. One leader said, "I would rather run into a brick wall than stand looking at it and try to figure out how to go around it." While in some ways this approach sounds like an admirable trait, it is a dangerous way to lead. Some brick walls are too thick, too large, or too complicated to just go running into them.

As a word of caution, coordination is not a conflict management technique that a leader can use to produce a "gotcha" moment. Leaders should never orchestrate the management of conflict to catch someone or a group in error. While a finely orchestrated plan may identify flaws in perspectives, errors in judgment, or other inaccuracies, the goal is not to point out people's wrongs. Coordination is about using activities and events to bring about the best resolution possible.

One leader had been asked to colead a special program within the large corporation where she was employed. She had a great track record of success. She led a large team of individuals who directly reported to her, and each of them highly regarded her. When she was given this project, she embraced it with enthusiasm. In tandem with the other coleader, she hired the right people to work in the program, built the partnerships she needed to make it successful, and diligently monitored its implementation and early progress.

Several months into the program, tension started to develop. The program had three employees. Two of the employees reported to this leader. The other employee reported to the coleader. The issue was that the three employees were being told different things and advised on different methods, protocols, and procedures for making things happen.

At first the tension was minimal mainly because of the three employees. The three had a great working relationship and were able to work through the differences. As a year was closing in, the tension was increasing and little by little growing into full-fledged conflict. As the employees gave reports to their supervisors, the coleaders, they included some of the conflicted situations they were facing. This in turn created tension between the coleaders. It was a situation that appeared to be escalating and putting the program at risk.

The leader who supervised the two employees recognized that something had to be done. If the program was going to remain viable and if they were going to keep good employees, the coleaders were going to have to address this distribution-of-power issue. The leader in question started coordinating the management of the conflict. She consulted the advice of a trusted colleague. She met with the two employees who reported directly to her and then the other employee. She met with the other coleader and discussed their differences. She developed what she thought was a reasonable and feasible plan of action for moving forward.

Once she had her plan prepared, she proposed the changes to the other coleader, who agreed with her conclusions. After this, they shared it with the executive leadership for approval and then passed it down to the three employees. The changes were received well. The lines of communication, responsibility, and accountability were clearly drawn. Each coleader knew the part of the program for which he or she was responsible. Each of the three employees had defined roles and knew to whom he or she reported. The coleaders agreed on certain protocols and procedures and left those undecided up to the respective coleader to determine.

What this leader did was recognize the need to coordinate a resolution that eliminated the tension and conflict. Her savvy leadership in orchestrating a plan saved this program and made the work environment enjoyable for all. The program took on a new life and continued for a couple more years until the need was no longer present.

Coordination is simply the idea of organizing, planning, or orchestrating a conflict management process in a way that brings about the best resolution possible. It is an intentional choice that a leader makes to work openly or behind the scenes to set the stage for the conflict to be managed. It is a conflict management technique that seeks the specific outcomes the leader deems are in the best interest of the organization or those involved.

MANAGING CONFLICT
with COOPERATION

■ The executive committee of a board of directors for a not-for-profit agency was meeting to discuss a very delicate issue. There was a situation occurring in the agency that was prompting a great deal of alarm, much scrutiny, and a call to action. The executive committee took responsibility for resolving the issue and started meeting to explore the matter and hopefully develop a plan of action. The consensus was that something had to be done, sooner rather than later, to address this conflicted situation or the agency could be in dire straits in the future.

All of the members of the executive committee were leaders representing diverse backgrounds and professions. They were bringing their collective expertise in leadership, management, crisis intervention, human resources, and more, to the table. All of them handled themselves with professional demeanor. Individual attitudes, the tones of vocabulary, and body language modeled professional expectations. There was mutual trust and respect for one another. Each felt valued. The meetings were conducted in an appropriate manner. While everyone wished these meetings could have been avoided, everyone felt comfortable with the way each interacted and the way the meetings were managed.

Perhaps one of the reasons the meetings went so well was the foundation on which they got started. At the very first meeting, one of the business leaders brought a one-page document that he distributed to participants. It was a simple list of ground rules for meetings that he uses with his company. He distributed the document, read through it, and asked if everyone could agree to adhere to the ground rules throughout the process. Everyone was in consensus that the ground rules were a great way to put boundaries on the conversation, stay focused, demonstrate integrity, and be equitable. They conducted the meetings accordingly.

For several months these professionals met and discussed the issue at hand. Not one time did someone get upset, make threats, cast blame, or try to sabotage the meetings. Every meeting was focused and on point. Each participant knew the work that needed to be accomplished and was committed to finding a palatable resolution for the agency.

These organizational leaders were able to process the issue that was adversely impacting the agency, reach consensus, and develop a recommended plan of action for the board. While their conversations were difficult and their recommendation significant, they worked together as one unit with a passion for the agency they were serving. One could say they modeled cooperation as each worked in tandem with the other to find the right resolution.

The Use of Cooperation

The use of cooperation in conflict management is the idea of people working together to resolve or manage the conflict. It may be in a manner as just described, with a professional team seeking to resolve an issue for an organization. It may also be a situation where two or more individuals are in conflict and a leader uses cooperation to help the conflicting parties work through the issue and find a solution.

Cooperation seeks to find solutions in the most peaceful and equitable ways possible. Distinctively different from other conflict management techniques, cooperation focuses heavily on getting conflicting parties to discuss the issue and collectively reach a resolution that is agreeable or acceptable to each of the parties. We may think of it as finding a middle ground or neutral territory.

The key to cooperation as a conflict management technique is engagement. Cooperation involves those who have a vested interest in the conflict and leads them through the process of working together toward a reasonable and peaceful solution. Stated simply, cooperation is the idea of getting people to work together in finding a resolution to the conflict.

In Acts 15, we read about the council at Jerusalem. Some individuals from Judea had arrived at Antioch and were teaching a custom to which others objected. They were teaching that according to Moses, a person could not be saved unless he was circumcised. This was extremely disturbing to the Gentiles in Antioch who had been saved but never circumcised. The Bible tells us that when Paul and Barnabas learned of this, they were "brought . . . into sharp dispute and debate with them" (v. 2). Paul and Barnabas traveled to Jerusalem with delegates from Antioch to meet with the Jerusalem elders and the apostles to sort out this issue.

The meeting must have been lengthy. The Bible says "after much discussion" (v. 7), implying that there were many opinions and ideas about how to handle the situation. Finally, Peter got up and addressed them. He articulated the case for salvation by grace for everyone (v. 11). Paul and Barnabas gave testimony to what God was doing through them in their journeys. Then James proceeded to clarify the issues to which they should be concerned. He declared they should not make it difficult for the Gentiles to turn to God.

On hearing the reports of Paul and Barnabas, along with the apostles' words, the Bible says, "Then the apostles and elders, with the whole church, decided" (v. 22). What they decided was to send representatives with Paul and Barnabas to Antioch with a letter outlining the conclusions to which they came. Essentially, they were clarifying the teaching about circumcision, confirming salvation by grace, and outlining what believers should be doing. The Bible says, "The people read it and were glad for its encouraging message" (v. 31).

This passage speaks to the spirit of cooperation. The delegates from Antioch, the elders from Jerusalem, the apostles, Paul, and Barnabas met to discuss the issue. While the initial response was to react through dispute and debate, they were able to have an open conversation about it with those who had the power to make definitive decisions. Following the compelling evidence of salvation by grace, all of them agreed on a cooperative resolution and personally delivered a letter to the Gentiles in Antioch stating the truth.

We cannot control when, where, and how conflict will arise. Conflict can happen at the most unexpected or inconvenient time. I doubt if Paul and Barnabas were waiting for a situation to break loose in Antioch; they were engaged in ministry when they learned something was happening. I doubt the Jerusalem elders, or even those in Antioch, were just waiting to solve the next big problem. Peter, James, or the other apostles probably didn't put dealing with this issue in their planners. Yet conflict was brewing.

Once the leaders learned of the conflict, they did go into action. They assembled those who needed to have a voice in the matter and began discussing it. With much conversation and thoughtful review, they were able to come to a resolution that allowed all of them to agree and address the conflict at hand.

Conflict is often hidden or masked by other issues. The people preaching circumcision in Antioch were following the laws of Moses as they had been taught. It is plausible they were not trying to usurp the Christian message of salvation by grace but simply defining salvation by what they believed to be right.

Some of the conflicted issues we face are often the result of uninformed people acting on inaccuracy. It is not always an intentional onslaught. In times like this, cooperation may work well. Cooperation provides the opportunity for everyone to have a voice and collectively find common ground for resolution.

Sometimes people's attitudes, even if they are not verbalized, are enough to influence their actions. By nature, we will likely conduct ourselves based on our beliefs, values, and learned mores. These factors influence our attitudes. Our attitudes often influence our responses to those things happening around us. When we perceive what is happening around us to be negative or threatening, our natural response is to react. We will often react to preserve what we believe is right. This can be viewed as conflict when it runs counter to what others are thinking and doing.

Cooperation as a conflict management technique is finding ways to bring differing views, values, opinions, beliefs, mores, and even attitudes to the same conversation. The goal is to work through differences and find a resolution with which everyone can live. It does not necessarily mean that everyone will ultimately agree with each other; however, it does mean everyone will work together.

Cooperation as a conflict management technique engages those who have a vested interest in the conflict. "Vested interest" is partially defined as "a special concern or stake in maintaining or influencing a condition, arrangement, or action especially for selfish ends."[1] Paul, Barnabas, the Antiochenes, the apostles, the elders—all had a vested interest in resolving the conflict in Antioch. People who are involved in a conflicted situation need to be included in managing or resolving the conflict. This is cooperation—getting all the parties who have a vested interest engaged in finding a resolution.

Components of Cooperation

Cooperation is working with those who are directly involved in the conflict to find a resolution with which everyone can live. Regardless of people's positions on an issue, the goal is to engage them and work through the conflict together. As a conflict management technique, cooperation is akin to finding consensus—a general agreement toward a solution to an issue or situation.

A tenured department leader for a large organization was seeking to find consensus among the individuals she supervised. The department had been given extra budget dollars to spend as it deemed appropriate. Obviously, there were several points of view on how the extra monies should be spent. This leader took the time to explain to the group that instead of a yea or nay vote, she wanted to reach consensus. She wanted to find a solution with which all of them could live, even though they may not totally agree with it. She was looking for cooperation.

Cooperation seeks to find solutions that build unity. It may be that not everyone is in total agreement with a particular solution, but each sees value in it and supports it. Even though not everyone will be in total agreement, consensus building looks for support and commitment so that everyone can be a team player. It really is a matter of being cooperative instead of oppositional.

Using cooperation as a conflict management technique should provide some form of mutual benefit for all parties involved. While some people may not totally agree with a solution, they believe that enough of their concerns were heard and incorporated into the resolution for them to live with it. Likewise, there may be those who were so overly expressive about an issue that in cooperation they are willing to scale back to make sure everyone is heard and satisfied with the resolution.

To the degree possible, cooperation seeks to be equitable to all. This may not mean everyone will benefit in equal proportion, but it does mean everyone will benefit in a way that is reasonable and fair. The objective is to find solutions where all walk away believing their voices were heard, their perspectives were considered, their concerns were addressed, and their problems were solved. At the same time, they need to do this without feeling they were taken advantage of or beat down in the process.

Cooperation may be thought of as a give-and-take process. Some people give up a little, and others take a little. In some ways, we may think of it as differing parties meeting somewhere in the middle. This process occurs with civility and compromise until both parties can reach a consensus that leads to a viable resolution. It does not mean everyone gets everything he or she wanted, but it does mean everyone can live with the outcome.

Cooperation is a lot like negotiation. Simply stated, it may be; however, it is probably the soft side of negotiation. Negotiation is more of a formal process for arriving at acceptable terms. Employment contracts are negotiated. The purchase of a house is negotiated. Cooperation has more to do with consensus building and less to do with contractual relations. Cooperation seeks to find a resolution where people can find unity around the solution, even if they may not agree with every part of it.

Cooperation is kind of like exchange theory. In exchange theory people consider the cost and return before deciding if a product, solution, or answer is worth the investment. If a person walks into a Quick Mart to purchase a twenty-ounce bottle of water and the price is $5.79, the person must decide if that bottle of water is worth the price. The person knows it is significantly higher than many other places; however, the decision may be made on the basis of multiple factors: (1) how thirsty the person is, (2) when the person last had something to quench the thirst, (3) how much money the person has, and (4) how long it will be until the person can expect to get another bottle of water. There could be additional considerations that go into this decision. The bottom line comes down to whether the cost is worth the return?

If the cost of giving up something is equal to or less than the value of what someone is getting in return, then the investment may be a good one. If it is not, the person may need to give more consideration before electing to do it. Cooperation is much like this. It is helping those in conflict decide what they can give up and what they can expect in return. Since the process is give-and-take, or exchange theory, it is about helping everyone involved find middle ground so that consensus can be reached. Not everyone will get the same benefit, but everyone will be able to live with what he or she is getting out of it.

There was a social service agency that was located in a historic building built prior to 1900. When the organization that built the building no longer needed it, it repurposed the building and leased it to this agency. Over the years, the agency grew, added services and staff, and for all practical purposes had nearly outgrown the building. In spite of this, the agency continued to make the best of the situation, attempting to fulfill its mission in the community.

There was a small kitchen in this building that the staff used as a kitchen for making coffee and storing supplies. The kitchen also had a refrigerator, stove, and microwave. The room was not really large enough to be a break room, since it was wall-to-wall cabinets or appliances. The fact is, there was very little room for anything else to be in the kitchen without taking up much of the limited floor space.

For years the agency had a table in this kitchen. It was not a large table, but in that kitchen, even a small table seemed to own the middle of the floor. One day, the executive director decided to move the table. He made this decision without discussing it with anyone. Needless to say, not everyone was pleased. While most agreed the extra floor space was nice, some liked the table in the kitchen.

The table in the kitchen became the topic of an ongoing discussion for several weeks as people weighed in on the matter. There were many points of view, some very valid. There were times the table was missed. There were other times when getting in the cabinets made one appreciate not having to move the table.

Finally, two staff members came to the executive director wanting to discuss the table issue again. The two staff members presented their case on how the table served a specific need once a week when their program hosted a certain activity. For this reason alone, they felt it was important to have the table in the kitchen. They boldly asked if the table could be replaced.

The three of them explored the issue further, looking for some solution. Using cooperation, the executive director tried to find consensus around various options. Finally, they found a solution, a little give-and-take on both sides. The program would purchase a small folding table comparable in size to the one that was removed from the kitchen. On days when the referenced activity was in the building, the staff would put the table up in the kitchen. The remainder of the time it would be broken down and stored, freeing up space for most of the week so that everyone could fully use the kitchen.

This solution was amenable to everyone. While not everyone totally agreed with this decision, everyone could accept it. In spite of the unintentional conflict the executive director created by moving the table, the result was a consensus with which he and all of the staff could live.

Cooperation begins with engaging those who are directly involved. It is about building consensus through the soft negotiation of giving and taking. It is seeking a solution with which everyone can live, even if he or she does not totally agree with every aspect of it. The goal of cooperation is to create buy-in, support, and commitment to seeing that the resolution agreed on will be implemented and carried out as planned.

Cooperation is a great conflict management technique. It affords the leader the opportunity to address the conflict directly and engage those who are involved. It involves a peaceful process of finding acceptable resolutions that everyone involved can accept and support.

MANAGING CONFLICT
with COLLABORATION

■ There was a community-ministry organization that served a broad geographical region in the state where it was located. With over twenty programs, the organization was touching thousands of lives annually. It was a great organization, a great place to work, a great place to volunteer to serve others, and a great place to get services. The organization had a long and rich history of positive influence in the communities it served.

One of the programs with which the organization part-
nered was a program serving center-city children. After school,
children were invited to the neighborhood center for tutoring,
activities, and a meal. For approximately two hours from the
time school dismissed until about five thirty, children would
study, play educational games, and enjoy dinner. They were in
a safe environment and were being fed a nutritious meal.

As that program evolved, the organization was successful
in obtaining grant money to help fund the program. The local food bank provided most of the food, but the cost of the
staff and supplies took additional monies that the grant funding
provided. One year, after a successful period of grant funding,
the organization learned that its largest grant would not be re-
newed. There were multiple reasons, but the bottom line was
that the organization was going to lose a significant percentage
of its financial resources.

The organization believed the program was worthy of con-
tinuation but also knew it needed to find additional resources to keep the program going or find a new way of making it
happen. The organization discussed its options and concluded
that financially it could not sustain the program the way it was
currently being delivered. The organization decided it would
begin talking to other community organizations about partnering with them to serve this need.

Several individual meetings occurred with various community organizations to ascertain interest in a partnership. Two
organizations expressed interest and volunteered to discuss it
further. After a few months of conversations and planning, a
partnership was born. One organization made four recreation-
al-type buildings available to serve children in this program.
Not only did this organization make the facilities available,

but it refurbished them, including state-of-the-art kitchens. That same organization repurposed a van for transporting food between sites. A second organization, which already offered after-school programming, volunteered to use its staff and volunteers to run the sites, work with the children, and serve the meals. This organization also dedicated a building to serve as a warehouse for food and supplies. The food bank continued to provide the food, increasing the amounts provided to serve the additional children. The original organization continued to coordinate the program, serve as the fiscal agent, and solicit grant funding for the services being offered.

This partnership dramatically changed the way after-school services were offered to center-city children in that community. In a matter of a few months the program went from one site to four sites and more than quadrupled the number of children being served. The financial resources required to operate this program were reduced as partnering organizations filled the need. Every organization was able to use its strengths and resources to meet a community need. This was a true partnership and collaboration.

Stephen Covey, in his *7 Habits of Highly Effective People*, encourages leaders to seek win-win solutions.[1] He distinguishes these from other forms of resolutions in which someone loses and someone wins. In win-win, everyone wins and there are no losers. This is the essence of true collaboration; people and entities coming together in ways that create solutions in which everyone wins. The partnership that evolved was collaboration at its finest—everyone won.

Collaboration is the idea of working jointly for the common good of all. It is more than a give-and-take negotiation. It is seeking a resolution in which everyone comes out on top and feels like a winner. It moves the pendulum from the negotiation approach of "I will, if you will" to "we can together."

In conflict management, collaboration is the optimal scenario. Generally speaking, conflict implies there are at least two sides to an issue or situation. Typically, this means there are people on both sides. Opposite sides implies opposing ideas and opinions. Collaboration seeks to find the common ground between sides, use the best of both, and arrive at a conclusion where everyone has contributed to the resolution.

In Acts 6, there is an account of people complaining about the distribution of food to the widows:

In those days when the number of disciples was increasing, the Hellenistic Jews among them complained against the Hebraic Jews because their widows were being overlooked in the daily distribution of food. So the Twelve [apostles] gathered all the disciples together and said, "It would not be right for us to neglect the ministry of the word of God in order to wait on tables. Brothers and sisters, choose seven men from among you who are known to be full of the Spirit and wisdom. We will turn this responsibility over to them and will give our attention to prayer and the ministry of the word." (Vv. 1-4)

Conflict was present. The Hellenistic Jews were complaining against the Hebraic Jews. The issue—the Hellenistic widows were not receiving their share of the distribution of food. The implication is that they were being slighted or overlooked. This was upsetting the Hellenistic Jew, who were concerned about the well-being of their widows. So they complained.

No doubt, there were two perspectives here. The Hebraic Jews may not have been doing this on purpose, but the perception was that equity was lacking. The widows were feeling the real impact, since they were not receiving their fair share of food. While the scripture passage does not say the widows were complaining, somehow the Hellenistic Jewish leaders knew about it. Issues may run deeper and be much more complex than they appear on the surface. Regardless, there was a problem.

The apostles moved into action. They called all of the disciples, those believers who were Christians, and began to discuss the situation. They proposed a win-win solution. The disciples were to consider electing seven qualified men who were filled with the Holy Spirit and demonstrated wisdom. These seven would be assigned leadership roles and charged with the responsibilities of overseeing the distribution of food. This in turn would free the apostles up to focus on the main thing—"prayer and the ministry of the word" (v. 4).

The apostles clearly demonstrated how a successful collaboration considers all aspects of a situation. They heard and took seriously the complaints of the Hellenistic Jews. On some level, they probably recognized that their commitment to "prayer and the ministry of the word" was leaving them limited time to administrate the distribution of food. While they worked hard to do everything that needed to be done, some widows were being neglected.

In an effort to seek a win-win solution, the apostles put together a team of middle managers who could focus solely on the distribution of food. Rather than randomly appoint people, they permitted the body of believers to elect the seven men who could best serve in this role. They gave the people, even those who were complaining, a voice in the solution. Once this team was in place, the apostles focused their attention on the more apostolic functions of ministry.

This collaboration resulted in many positive outcomes: (1) the people complaining were heard, (2) more people got involved in ministry, (3) the elected leadership were from among the people, (4) the widows' needs were met, and (5) the apostles' time was freed up so they could focus on the ministry to which they were called. The apostles' leadership enabled them to address this conflict in a collaborative way, leading to a positive resolution for everyone involved.

Components of Collaboration

Collaboration begins with truly hearing the voices of others involved. When the Hellenistic Jews complained, the apostles listened. For legitimate collaboration to occur, everyone involved needs to be at the table and his or her voice needs to be heard. It is too easy to jump to conclusions or assume we know what people are thinking without consulting them or actively listening to them. People need the opportunity to tell their side of the story and express what they are feeling.

Working toward collaboration requires active listening skills. Active listening includes paying attention, demonstrating that you are listening, providing feedback, deferring judgment, and responding appropriately.[2] It is important that the leader hear what the other person is saying and then understands, from the other person's perspective, what the real issue is that is causing the conflict. If a leader cannot actively listen, he or she will never truly understand what is at stake.

Once others have had the opportunity to provide input, the leader can begin to make informed decisions and judgments. If this involves telling another side of the story, the leader has the foundation on which to build. Covey described it as seeking first to understand and then to be understood.[3] It is very difficult for a leader to manage conflict if he or she does not know the whole story. Again, it is a matter of good assessment. Getting people involved in the resolution or management of the conflict is extremely important. The apostles recruited seven men who could step up and take on responsibility to ensure the issue was resolved. Involving others has a twofold benefit. First of all, it adds value by giving them a meaningful way to connect and be involved. Second, it creates a vested interest in the right outcome. People who have a vested interest in the process will usually see things from a different perspective.

Bringing those who are creating the conflict, if it is appropriate, into the process of managing the conflict is a powerful way to get buy-in. It is hard for people to continue to create controversy, stir up trouble, or identify problems when they are in the midst of the solution and possibly providing some level of guidance or leadership.

There was a pastor who really struggled with people continuously making suggestions, recommending changes, or telling him what he should be doing about something. In an effort to let them know he was hearing them and yet not invest a lot of time chasing everything they proposed, he started responding to the naysayers by suggesting they should join a committee, volunteer to assist, or participate in some other way. He encouraged them to get involved and help resolve the problem. Many elected to quit bringing up so many issues. A few did get involved, and for them it was amazing how different things looked from another perspective.

One of the beautiful things about collaboration is that generally it leads to amazing outcomes. The apostles were confident that the widows would not be overlooked in the distribution of food with this new system in place. The system was specifically designed to address the specific need in question. Conflict is best averted when the specific issue or situation is addressed.

If a leader is facing conflict and attempts to address the symptoms instead of the real issue, the conflict will likely not be managed well and probably never be resolved. Too often, leaders are tempted to find the path of least resistance in dealing with conflict in order to avoid offending, hurting, or adversely impacting the organization or the people involved. The question that must be asked is, "Are those leaders doing justice to the issue?" Is this the right way to handle a situation?

Sometimes cutting to the core and addressing the real issue will be the best way to manage the conflict in the long run. It may be a little more risky, a little more painful, but in the end the issue is dealt with and not just the symptoms. The focus needs to be on the real issue at hand.

The apostles could have accused the Hellenistic Jews of being complainers, being greedy, having a grudge against the Hebraic Jews, or any number of things. If that would have been the assumption they made and used to address the subsequent symptom, they would have missed the mark totally. By making sure the heart of the issue was addressed, they successfully managed the conflict at hand. While we will never know for sure, it seemed as though that was the end of the issue.

Good conflict management frees up a leader's time and focus. The apostles were able to concentrate on their particular ministry. They did not have to juggle their priestly functions with administrative details once they implemented a plan of action. They delegated the responsibility of the distribution of food and moved on to other leadership tasks.

A leader can spend a lot of time trying to manage conflict. This is even truer if the leader is addressing the symptoms instead of the root of the issue. Consequently, the leader may get frustrated, discouraged, drained, and possibly lose perspective. It is even possible to feel that the mundane activity of constantly dealing with conflict is robbing the creative energy that could be going into the ministry of the Word. What impact does this have on the leader's prayer life? For what is he or she always praying about when the environment is full of conflict?

Managing conflict by listening to those who are involved, engaging them in finding a solution, and making sure the core of the issue is what is being addressed is the most beneficial way to ensure the leader can remain focused on the primary tasks of ministry. The leader will spend less time dealing with conflict when these components are incorporated into the management of the conflict. The result will be a collaboration in which everyone comes out winning.

Truths about Collaboration

While the process of collaboration seems fairly straightforward, it is one of the hardest conflict management techniques to implement. Confrontation or complacency are easier and require less work for engagement. Communication, cooperation, and coordination require significantly more work. The outcomes will be different depending on the technique used. Collaboration is the only conflict management technique where everyone feels like a winner.

Knowing this, it behooves the leader to invest the necessary time and energy in performing a good assessment, identifying the strengths of the situation or people involved, and working toward outcomes that are beneficial for everyone. This may require multiple meetings or conversations over coffee or lunch.

It will require significant time in prayer and waiting on God, seeking wisdom and direction.

At the same time, collaboration is the most rewarding of the conflict management techniques. A leader may feel a sense of "release" when he or she confronts someone and gets something out in the open. Likewise, a leader may feel good about finding a resolution through another technique such as cooperation. Collaboration is the only technique where all people involved feel they are valued, their voices are heard, the need is met, and the outcome is more than satisfactory.

For leaders who seek to maintain integrity, build credibility, and develop a systemic infrastructure for providing true leadership, collaboration is the best way to go. When people see the leader respond to conflict in a way that is methodical, equitable, and authentic, they are much more likely to respond with respect and trust. People follow leaders who demonstrate their ability to lead through the conflict.

Conflict often has tentacles of emotions, perceptions, and memories. People feel, think, and remember things that happened, what was said, or who did what. These things do not automatically dissipate the moment a conflict is resolved. There may be additional work in addressing some of these issues, or over time complacency may work. On the other hand, when people see the spirit and outcome of a collaborative approach, it is much more likely that any lingering tentacles will be addressed indirectly.

An additional benefit of collaboration as a conflict management technique is its systemic impact. Unlike the other models, collaboration seeks the common good. While a few individuals may be directly affected, the result or outcome influences the whole organization and everyone in it. Everyone may not be aware of what happened, but the positive ramifications will have a ripple effect throughout the organization. The organization will be stronger, more reputable, and healthier in the long run.

One midsize community was struggling with serving those who were by definition homeless. Some were true transients who were passing through because of the geographical location of the community and its proximity to main thoroughfares. Others were individuals who for any number of reasons were "down on their luck" and without a safe, standardized place to reside.

Two neighboring communities had homeless shelters. Both were often full. While some individuals would take advantage of the services those shelters offered, others refused. Generally, these were individuals who found themselves evicted or displaced because of an emergency, such as a fire, or some other circumstance, such as car trouble while traveling and lacking the means to get a motel room. Many of these individuals did not want to seek the services of a shelter, so they sought other options.

Often these individuals would visit local churches seeking money to pay for a motel room, a meal, a tank of gas, or something similar. When the clergy started comparing notes, they were surprised at the number of people they were serving collectively. As the clergy continued to compare notes, they learned several of the individuals were going from church to church, night to night, asking for emergency funds to help. Some of the individuals were making rounds through the community continuously looking for assistance.

This community was blessed with two faith-based agencies that provided emergency assistance to those in need. Individuals and families could visit one of these agencies and request services for shelter, food, clothing, and, in some cases, medical needs. Both agencies had limits on the services that could be provided. Like the churches, people were visiting both agencies and maximizing the services.

During one ministerial meeting that included personnel from the two agencies, the issue of so many people seeking assistance was brought up. The sentiment was that something had to be done. There was a sense of general frustration. The current way of doing things was draining resources from both the churches and the agencies. Likewise, some thought the current structure was probably enabling those who were seeking services. The two agencies agreed to take the lead and attempt to address the problem.

The agency representatives invited the two clergy who were being affected the most to join the committee. The group met a few times, discussed the issue, assessed the community needs and resources, identified the strengths in the current system, identified the gaps in the current system, and proposed a plan of action. The goal was to serve those who had need, be good stewards of the resources in the community, ease the burden on the churches and the agencies, and to some extent reduce fraudulent activity.

This outcome was a collaboration that everyone bought into and committed to follow. To briefly summarize the plan, one agency agreed to be the clearinghouse for all people wanting the services. Churches and agencies would refer everyone seeking emergency shelter to this agency. The agency would do an assessment and, depending on the need, arrange or provide the services necessary. The agency would in turn communicate with the churches and other agency on the resources needed for this to happen. Anyone could refer people to the homeless shelters, but only this one agency would communicate with the local hotels and motels. If someone was seeking services after normal business hours, he or she was referred to the police department, who would in turn contact the agency. The outcome was a single source of service delivery that was supported by the community at large.

What happened in this community was a true collaboration. When the issue was identified and became a point of discussion at the ministerial meeting, the leaders went into action. They appointed a committee of those most affected, assessed the situation, and addressed the specific need. The outcomes were people's needs still being met, a systemic solution that was beneficial for everyone, and the clergy spending more time attending to the work of ministry. It was a win-win.

Collaboration as a conflict management technique is powerful. It is the most challenging way to handle conflict, but it is also the most rewarding. By including others and addressing the specific issue, conflict can be managed in a way that gives people a voice, meets their need, and frees up the leader to the priestly functions of ministry. When the goal is the common good of everyone involved, everyone wins.

CHOOSING A TECHNIQUE

■ A middle-aged senior pastor was facing a situation he was not sure how to handle. A young man had started attending the church. The pastor knew of this man and that he had a sordid background. The young man was raised in the church but during his youthful years turned to behaviors that contradicted Christian faith. This young man was now in his late twenties, single, and searching for answers to life's questions. So, he started attending church again.

While the young man seemed sincere, several in the church were concerned. They expressed appreciation for his sensitivity to turning to the church, but they doubted his transformation. Their doubt seemed to be a cover for their own fears as they questioned this man's past and wondered what could happen in the future. While they did not want to turn him away, they did not truly embrace him.

What made the situation more challenging was that this man's sister and her husband faithfully attended and supported the church. As a matter of fact, they provided some of the strongest leadership in the church. They, too, did not condone the man's past, but he was family and was back in the church after many years of wandering astray. They strived to make him feel welcome, loved, and included.

After a while, to engage him and help him feel valued his sister invited him to work with her in one of the ministries of the church. It seemed so simple. He would be with her all of the time. She would provide supervision and mentoring. He would be an extra person to assist. The problem was that others in the church did not see it this way. How could the church permit a person with his background to be involved at that level?

People started talking. The conversations moved from informal discussions among faithful church people to a proposed agenda item for the board meeting. The situation was becoming very controversial. As much as those involved tried to keep it quiet, it soon became common knowledge. There were opinions and attitudes on both sides of the issue.

The pastor was totally perplexed and uncertain how to approach the matter. He wanted to see this man continue in his journey of faith. The pastor believed in the sister and what she committed to do to assist her brother. The pastor calculated the risks and placed safeguards throughout to ensure the situation could be managed, including talking to the man about expectations. On the other side were the other church leaders who were expressing the strong opinion that the church should not permit this man to continue working with the ministry. While they stated they were okay with him attending church, they were keeping him at arm's length.

The pastor stood at a crossroads and needed to make a decision about how to address and handle this. Full-on conflict was brewing. It was going to erupt into a situation where only adverse outcomes could be anticipated if he did not intervene with some form of conflict management. As the pastor was beginning to choose a conflict management style and lay the groundwork to begin the process, the situation resolved itself. The man left the church.

Deciding to Engage

One of the most difficult decisions a leader makes is the decision to get involved in an issue or situation where conflict is ensuing. Unlike the young, unlearned preacher who stated "I am always looking for a good rumble," most of us prefer to avoid conflict. We find it time consuming, energy draining, and spiritually exhausting. In addition, we know that we run the risk of harming relationships with those involved and in some cases adversely impacting our leadership and possibly our tenure as leader. With the associated risks, it is safer not to engage unless we absolutely must.

We also must be honest and state that there will be times when we do not have a choice and must engage in a conflicted situation. As much as we would like to avoid it, the conflict is such that it is going to require our involvement as the leader. Without our intervention, things could get out of hand and turn ugly, people could get hurt, the organization could suffer, or any number of other negative consequences. How do we make that decision? How do we know when we need to engage? When do we get involved?

The best way to think about this is by thinking of a pyramid. A pyramid is a triangular-shaped form in which the bottom is wide and the sides tilt in to reach a point at the top. Divide the pyramid into three sections: the pinnacle (or the very top point), a midsection, and the lower section or base. Each of these areas will represent a level of criticalness for intervening in conflict.

At the point of the pyramid are absolute nonnegotiable standards, truths, practices, and more. These are the things the organization will not and cannot compromise. These are the tried-and-true absolutes that have stood the test of time and continue to stand; they serve as the foundational and guiding principles of the organization. Regardless of what may come, who the leader is, what issue arises, the pinnacle of the pyramid represents the nonnegotiable items of the organization.

An example of a nonnegotiable may be scriptural truth. By this, we are talking about tenets of the faith and not nuances of opinion. We believe the Scriptures to be true and right. No matter the situation, the Word of God should not be misconstrued or misrepresented. This makes it a nonnegotiable. It clearly rests at the top of the pyramid.

Other things that may be near the top of the pyramid include vision, mission, and core values. These are typically hammered out and adopted by a legislative body to provide a conceptual and operational framework for the organization. Generally, these remain in place until formal action is taken to revise them. On an ongoing basis, these kinds of things cannot be compromised without the organization finding itself bouncing around without direction and casting a shifting shadow.

There may be other foundational elements that an organization holds as near and dear that are really nonnegotiable for the organization. For example, an organization that was born in response to a specific need or tragedy may be committed to serving that population or geographical area regardless of what changes around them. I know of a Christian counseling center that was born out of the grief of two families and their teenagers. The organization made a commitment that it would serve all youth who wanted help regardless of finances. Through the years this has been a nonnegotiable.

Moving down from the pinnacle, we enter the center part of the pyramid. This is the area where items are fairly structured and set; however, with appropriate action they may be modified or adjusted. Typically, items in this area are not negotiated regularly; however, the possibility of negotiating them exists, and change can be made without adversely affecting the core purposes of the organization.

The middle part of the pinnacle may include organizational structure, service times, employee/employer relations, performance expectations, policies, and curriculum. These are established and provide the framework for what we do but with appropriate action may be changed to meet the current demands of the organization and better serve our clients.

The bottom of the pyramid consists of those things that are fairly negotiable. These may be preferences, likes, conveniences, creature comforts, and similar affective influencers. These items may modify something we do, see, or expect but at the end of the day do not compromise the purposes of the organization or fundamentally change how we do what we do.

A simple example is a church that has a fellowship time between services. As people are coming and going and transitioning to Sunday school, coffee and pastries are served. This time is designed to encourage fellowship with others and to provide refreshments. Some may prefer a particular name-brand coffee be served, while others may simply choose a store brand. Both are coffee. The brand is simply a matter of preference. The type of coffee does not change the purposes or function of the church. While some may be very adamant, the fact is, this is a negotiable.

Knowing where an issue rests on the pyramid helps the leader ascertain to what extent he or she should engage in the conflict. Choosing the brand of coffee is really a decision that should be left to someone else and to which a leader should respond by using complacency. Even if the leader prefers a name brand, it is not an issue worth any more energy than drinking a cup of coffee and being thankful for it.

On the other hand, if something is being proposed that fundamentally changes the way an organization does what it does, then the leader may need to choose a conflict management technique that best addresses it. If someone is proposing and recruiting support for changes to policies about how clients are served, this is significant. A leader may need to look at communication or cooperation to work through the issue. At some point, it will require the support of the legislative body. That body will arrive at a decision after having heard all of the facts and rationale. Complacency and confrontation are not good options for decisions like this.

Those items at the pinnacle are to some extent fixtures of the organization. In some ways, these items create the tapestry that states who an organization is and what it does. They are the bedrock of existence. While they may be changed, this should only occur after thorough discussion, broad support, and sincere prayer. Changes here redefine purpose and mission. Managing conflict in this arena demands cooperation at the very least but is better served with collaboration.

Leaders must decide when an issue needs their attention and to what extent. Not every issue will demand the engagement of the leader. Any issue at risk of compromising a nonnegotiable demands the leader's attention. Regardless of the situation or issue, leaders should give careful thought to a conflicted situation, bathe it in prayer, and cautiously engage it if necessary.

Knowing Oneself

In the same vein, leaders need to know themselves and what their core values are for life and service. As a leader, I want to model Christlike character. I have some core values that drive every decision and commitment I make. I know to what degree I will be complacent or tolerate some things, and I know where I will not compromise. My awareness of who I am and what I value becomes a filter for when and how I respond to those things around me.

Authentic leadership is the wisdom of a leader to take who he or she is and overlay that with the organization's vision, mission, and values. When these two arenas meet, authentic leadership takes place. If there is a disconnect, the leader, organization, or both will be perplexed, confused, or conflicted. There is great value in a leader serving an organization whose core purpose for being aligns with his or her values.

The more authentic the leadership is, the more authentic the conflict management will be. If there is a mismatch between leadership and the organization, it will be more difficult to navigate through conflict. There is a risk of bias, misaligned focus, and differences in anticipated outcomes. Leaders who find themselves in this scenario may be tempted to use a more complacent or aggressive conflict management technique than necessary. This increases risk and diminishes the probability of successful resolution.

A brand-new pastor moved to his first church. The church consisted of a small number of people in a very modest building, but the spirit and attitude of the people were amazing. The building was in need of some TLC (tender loving care), and so the pastor along with leaders in the church put together a plan and started doing some things to improve the appearance of the facilities and the ambience of the sanctuary.

Hanging on the wall in the front of the sanctuary, behind the pulpit, was a cross. It was small and had a stained-glass look, and its bright color stood out among the other decor in the sanctuary. As the pastor and leaders were sorting items in storage, they found the original wooden cross. It was larger, blended with the decor, and matched the period the sanctuary was built.

Discussion ensued about the possibility of replacing the stained-glass-looking cross with the original cross. The pastor was probably the most verbal and most passionate about it, since his preference was clearly the wooden cross. Fortunately, the pastor had the wisdom to do an assessment of the situation before replacing the cross. In the days that followed, the pastor learned that one of the saints of the church had a son who made the stained-glass-looking cross for the church. It was a labor of love and a gift of gratitude to the church.

The pastor was wise enough to see this as a negotiable. He was in touch with his own core values enough that he knew this matter would not change the purposes or mission of the church. While he preferred the wooden cross, it was not an issue he was going to push. The church kept the wooden cross stored for historical and nostalgic reasons, but the smaller, stained-glass-looking cross remained in the sanctuary. No one will ever know, but the reality is that it probably did not change the worship experience and what God did in the hearts of those whose lives were touched.

WHEN TO NEGOTIATE

■ A young pastor had worked hard to schedule a series of revival services for the church. He planned it over a year ahead, confirmed the evangelist, and arranged for the special music. Through the pastor's lens, this was not going to be an ordinary revival. He was expecting God to move in mighty ways in the hearts and lives of the people. Likewise, he was counting on new people coming to know the Lord before the week would end. This revival was going to be something great!

One of the plans the pastor made was to have a group of young people who did both volunteer service and music ministry there on a Saturday before revival services started on Sunday. The plan was that during the day on Saturday the young people would go door-to-door in the community and pass out flyers about a Saturday night concert and the upcoming revival services. The plan was to invite people to hear them sing and then come back for revival.

Everything was going as planned leading up to that Saturday. The pastor had all the details worked out for Saturday's outreach initiative. The evangelist would be arriving Saturday afternoon, ready to start services on Sunday morning. The song evangelist would be arriving Sunday afternoon to lead the music for the rest of the week. Everything was falling into place—that is, until Saturday morning.

Saturday morning when the group of young people did not show up, the pastor contacted the sponsoring organization using its emergency phone number. He thought maybe they were lost, were running late, or had vehicle trouble. What he heard were these words: "The group members changed their minds, and they are not coming. We are sorry!" Needless to say, that did not sit well with the pastor. He asked the person on the other end of the line to repeat the words and then started asking questions, which the person could not answer.

After deciding he was not going to get anywhere, the pastor thanked the person on the phone for his time and hung up. He started calling the main numbers of the organization. Because it was a Saturday morning, he could not get an answer from any of the offices. After an hour or so he got very resourceful and found the home number for the leader of the organization. He called that number and spoke to the leader's wife. He explained the situation. She assured him she would pass it on to her husband when he returned.

In the meantime, the clock was ticking. He decided he could forgo the outreach efforts he had planned for the young people, since only the church people knew about it. The concert that evening was a different matter. The church had already advertised a special concert and needed to make it happen. The pastor contacted the song evangelist and inquired about his ability to come that afternoon and provide a concert that evening. Fortunately, the song evangelist just happened to already be in the area and agreed to provide the concert. The pastor was relieved that he had the concert covered but still bothered by what the organization did to the church.

The pastor was trying to regroup and get back to the spirit of revival. In the early afternoon, the office phone rang. The person on the end of the line identified himself as the assistant leader of the organization and wanted to know what in the world the young pastor was doing calling the leader's home. His exact words were, "You are too young a preacher to be making waves like this." The pastor was taken aback with his tone and implied accusation.

For the next five minutes or so, the pastor explained that he had planned a day of outreach, a concert, and a revival. He talked about how all of the services connected and what the church hoped to see from this effort. In a moment of boldness, he expressed great displeasure with the organization and its lack of follow-through. Since he was on a roll, he told the assistant leader he thought what they did was unprofessional and potentially detrimental to the church's view of the organization.

Once the assistant leader heard the whole story, he sincerely apologized. He then said he would have someone at the church in time for a concert that evening. The pastor thanked him for understanding and being willing to send an alternative; however, he declined the group because he had already worked out the concert details with the song evangelist. The assistant leader assured the pastor that this would never happen again and the organization would like the opportunity to send a group at another time. On this note the conversation ended, and the concert and revival went on as adjusted.

For years to come, the pastor remembered the words of that assistant leader, who said, "You are too young a preacher to be making waves." Does age, length of tenure, experience, or some other trait predetermine when a leader should respond to a conflicted situation? Absolutely not! Leaders need to respond to conflict when it is appropriate. Determining when it is appropriate may be one of the greatest challenges in conflict management.

The young pastor above responded to the conflict by using confrontation. He simply addressed the issue head-on and did what he had to do to find an acceptable resolution. Others may have handled it differently, but he did what he thought had to be done at the time. Knowing when to intervene and what technique to use is important, but understanding the principles of negotiation is just as important.

Realistically, the issues that are considered nonnegotiable are probably few. As previously noted, scriptural foundations are paramount. It is absolutely critical that Christlikeness be held as the standard. This includes integrity, honesty, treating others equitably, and serving those in need. It is important, especially for churches, that statements of faith be honored and observed. An organization that claims it is faith based needs to model the character, attitudes, and dispositions of faith. These may vary from tradition to tradition, but faith-based organizations need to be true to what they profess.

It is imperative to guard the vision, mission, and core values of the organization. As previously stated, if an organization waffles on these things, no one will know for what it really stands. Its influence will be diminished. Trust will be lost. Over time, there will be an erosion of credibility. An organization cannot compromise on those things that define its purpose for being or those things it holds true to how it fulfills its mission.

Conflict that is jeopardizing relationships or ministry may be viewed as nonnegotiable. If interpersonal relationships between parishioners or employees have escalated to a point where it is destroying harmony and unity, then it must be addressed. At this point it becomes a nonnegotiable because it is compromising the purposes of the organization. Likewise, if something is occurring that is hindering the organization from doing what it is designed to do, it becomes a nonnegotiable. It too must be addressed.

When conflict moves out of the organization into a broader arena, it becomes an issue that must be addressed. If employees start bad-mouthing an organization in public, it erodes confidence in the organization and may have detrimental consequences, such as diminished respect, reduced funding, and less community support. If parishioners are negative about their church or pastor, or if the pastor speaks ill against the church in his circle of friends, then it harms the church. Why would anyone want to attend or trust a church where the pastor or people are negative? Conflict that is transcending the boundaries of the organization must be managed.

Generally speaking, conflict that compromises the core tenets of the organization has to be addressed and managed.

If not, the conflict has the potential to destroy the organization over time. Conflict that is deteriorating relationships and causing division within the organization must be handled. In the same vein, if the conflict is moved to an external audience, it must be managed. All of these scenarios are nonnegotiable.

Now, before you take this at face value and quit reading to go address a conflict, please hear my heart. While I believe in managing conflict that compromises a nonnegotiable as just mentioned, I also believe in maintaining and preserving Christian character and witness. Another chapter deals with the leader's example, so just let me say that we have to be careful not to get so dragged into the conflict that we become part of the problem instead of the resolution. This is where choosing the appropriate conflict management technique, including confrontation, will help us.

Issues that are in the middle of the pyramid may be just as important but will probably be handled differently. A nonnegotiable leaves little room for options; the conflict must be addressed. By not addressing it, we place the organization at risk. Issues that are realistically in the midrange of the pyramid are very important and worthy of our attention but may not place the organization at risk. These issues are more a matter of function and practice. Consequently, we have the luxury of time, process, and opportunity to maximize the conflict management techniques used in midpyramid situations.

Conflicted situations at the bottom of the pyramid may be worth noting, but the leader may choose complacency as an appropriate response. Issues at the top of the pyramid demand our attention. Those issues at the bottom may not. We may be aware of them, but engaging at this level is really risky to the leader. As stated, leaders have to guard themselves and demonstrate Christian character. Sometimes the best way to do this is not to engage.

Guiding Principles

Generally speaking, leaders should take the path of least resistance to the extent it is possible. As stated, when issues arise that place the organization at risk, intervention is necessary. On the other hand, when the risk is low, intervention may not be necessary or we may choose an intervention that is low risk. Complacency is generally a feasible option when the risk is really low or the outcomes will not fundamentally change the organization's purpose or ability to fulfill its mission.

If a leader elects to engage in managing conflict, it should be handled in a timely and efficient manner. This does not mean a leader rushes into a situation. I would not adopt the philosophy of the leader previously mentioned who talked about running into brick walls (chap. 8). Addressing a situation in a timely manner means that after thorough assessment and planning, and bathing the situation in prayer, the leader appropriately responds.

It is easy to get sidetracked and allow an issue to grow into something larger than it really is. Likewise, some situations can easily sprout tentacles that spread throughout the organization. Proper conflict management should seek to address the central issue of the conflict and not allow it to fester or spread. Great effort should be exercised to ensure the focus is maintained on the real issue and not let other influencers impact the process. This is challenging, since peoples' attitudes, beliefs, and feelings will be expressed. A wise leader will be aware of these things and strive to keep the focus where it belongs.

Conflict needs to be managed within the boundaries of where it is occurring and with those who are directly involved.

For example, if an issue arises within a church board meeting and among the board members, it should be managed within the same context. This does not mean there may not be private conversations outside of meetings with those involved, but it does mean those involved are not talking about it with others who are not on the church board and even with those who may be on the board but are not involved.

Confidentiality is a key component in conflict management. Groups such as church boards, boards of directors, and employee groups should understand that confidentiality is an expectation. Some organizations even require individuals serving in leadership roles to sign confidentiality agreements. Unfortunately, sometimes we are dealing with conflict between people and in contexts where confidentiality is not a requirement. In situations like this, leaders need to remind those involved that maintaining confidentiality will better serve the conflict management process. It is detrimental to conflict management to have people talking about the conflict with those who are not involved.

When the Conflict Cannot Be Resolved

Occasionally leaders will be engaged in managing a conflicted situation that is not moving toward the desired resolution. For any number of reasons, it becomes apparent that the desired outcomes are not going to be reached. What do we do then? How do we continue to work with the people involved? How do we handle the situation moving forward? What will the impact be to the organization?

In situations like this the leader needs to remain faithful. Doing the right thing regardless of the outcome demonstrates the best of integrity and Christlike attitudes and behaviors. We still love the people even if we do not agree with the way they are handling a situation. We still have the best interest of the organization at heart. We continue to plan and strategically move with Christian compassion and focused objectives.

Sometimes we may have a situation where we just agree to disagree. An executive director and a program director were having ongoing conversations about a specific situation. They were on opposite sides of the issue. Both were competent and capable of making good decisions. Both respected and trusted the other. In the end, they agreed that they did not see this particular issue the same. They acknowledged they viewed it differently, agreed to disagree, and moved on to other things at hand. It was an amicable decision that did not hinder their working relationship or place the organization at risk.

There are many other conflicted situations where the answer is not this simple. Sometimes, a successful resolution may involve a legislative body, that is, a church board or board of directors, making a policy or procedural decision to which everyone within the organization must adhere. Sometimes the leader must make an executive decision and mandate adherence. Sometimes it is just a matter of enforcing existing policy or protocol with the expectation that everyone will follow it.

There are other times when those involved, even with the appropriate conflict management technique or enforcement of policy and standard operating procedure, will not allow resolution to occur. There may be multiple reasons for this, including attitudes, beliefs, convictions, understanding of policy, and feelings. Sometimes, people just refuse to change their position or action. When this occurs, leaders must determine if the continuance of this refusal will be detrimental to the organization. If not, then maybe the conflicted situation is not really conflict. If so, then more drastic measures need to be taken.

In employer and employee relations, leaders may need to exercise authority. This may mean an informal reprimand, formal documentation, or possibly terminating an employee's tenure. All of these options should only be done after the leader has exercised every other possible opportunity to redeem the situation and resolve any conflict. The leader needs be sure that he or she has acted with the right motives, practiced due diligence, and is under the divine direction of grace and compassion. Altering someone's life by this kind of intervention should not be taken lightly; however, leaders should not acquiesce from their responsibility if this is the decision that must be made.

When a leader is dealing with volunteers, parishioners, noncontractual associations, and similar relationships, conflicted situations become more challenging. A leader must think through the conflict management techniques and what will be most productive in the particular situation with which he or she is dealing. When the conflict cannot be resolved, a leader may need to turn to cooperation and find a working relationship that is palatable for everyone involved.

Occasionally a situation may be so severe that it requires a difficult conversation with a volunteer explaining why his or her service is not a good fit for the organization or in a particular role. A wise leader will be compassionate, specific, and redemptive. Offering to help find the volunteer another place of service within or without the organization is a kind gesture. If the leader cannot do this with a clear conscience, then it is best to be honest with the volunteer. There is inherent risk in dealing with a volunteer this way; however, sometimes it must be done to resolve conflicted situations and protect the organization.

When the conflict exists with parishioners, it is even more challenging. Sometimes the issue may be a person or group that is creating chaos and conflict. At other times it may be a dynamic reaction to existing leadership, including pastoral leadership, or the direction in which the church is headed. These issues are hard to sort out. As an issue is sorted out, the leader has to remember that he or she is dealing not only with an individual but also with the impact the situation will have on the body of believers in the church and the pastoral relationship. There are no easy answers!

A district leader once told a young pastor who was facing conflict in the church, "The people in the church were there before you arrived, and they will be there when you are gone." This district leader was advising the pastor to tread carefully through the situation. While pastors are expected to be church leaders, the truth is, they are called to serve and can only serve those who want to be served. When the resistance to pastoral leadership is such that it hinders the purpose and mission of the church, the pastor should perhaps seek another opportunity to serve.

On the other hand, there are those situations where the issue is clearly with an individual or small group, and finding a resolution besides the pastor leaving is in the best interest of the church. Church leaders will wrestle with how to handle situations like this when the best conflict management techniques have not worked to date and yet something has to be done. These situations will no doubt stir up trepidation in the heart of the leader. Intervention must be entered with prayer and after seeking the mind of God through his Word.

A younger pastor was dealing with such a situation in the church. At the last board meeting, a longtime member publicly challenged the pastor in front of the other board members. The pastor was leading the board in a visioning process when this board member did not agree with the board and directed his disagreement and frustration to the pastor. He insulted the pastor, accused him of poor leadership, and threatened to withhold his tithe and leave the church. This was not the first time the board member acted this way.

The other board members were appalled at the statements the one board member was making. They expressed appreciation for the pastor and the direction the visioning process was headed. The one board member was unrelenting and continued his rant. In the moment, the pastor seeing the disdain and discomfort of the other members addressed the board member by declaring, "This is God's church, he will build his church, and the gates of hell will not prevail against it" (see Matt. 6:18). He went on to inform the board member that this meant God could build his church with or without any one of them or their money. No doubt this was bold and probably not the best choice of responses, but it was effective.

The board member stood up and declared, "I have never had a pastor talk to me this way!" Then he turned and left. As he was leaving, one of the other board members spoke up and said, "Well, maybe it's about time one did!" You can guess the rest of the story. The man called the district leadership and resigned from the board, and he and his wife left the church and took their tithe with them.

The pastor was right with his biblical interpretation. You have to admire his faith. You may question the way he handled it; he did after the fact. The good news is, the remaining board stood with the pastor and pressed on being the church. God was faithful, in spite of the circumstances. The very next Sunday, a new young couple came to the church and from the get-go started tithing more than the board member who left.

Other situations are less confrontational but nevertheless just as critical. A middle-aged woman was struggling with her faith. She had faithfully attended the church for years, fulfilling every role no one else was willing to do. Her husband did not attend but supported her involvement. Over time, she became burned out. She expressed frustration that she had to do so much in the church while others refused to step up and serve.

After counseling the woman over a period of weeks, the pastor recognized that this woman needed a sabbatical to recover, regroup, and be revived. He suggested she step back from her responsibilities and just worship. She expressed concern that she could not do that because of others' expectations and how much there was to do. She suggested she attend church elsewhere for a few weeks, take a break, and then return with fewer responsibilities. The pastor agreed to the plan. He knew the risk that she may not return, but he also knew her salvation was more important.

The woman did take a break and attended another church those few weeks. When she returned, she was a different person. She was smiling, happy, and her faith had been restored. After a few more weeks, she once again talked to the pastor. She shared how the time at the other church was so enjoyable and such a time of spiritual growth. She stated that she was thinking about attending that church all of the time.

The words "attending that church all of the time" were not the words the pastor wanted to hear. He asked himself, "How could this church lose someone of her talent and faithfulness?" Yet the pastor knew that he could not hold her back. While disappointment loomed in his heart, he encouraged her to follow her heart and do what she believed the Lord wanted her to do. She left, joined the other church, and continued to grow in her faith. A few years later, she was heard testifying that the pastor of the church she left gave her the freedom to leave and find a place where she could grow. God is faithful and works in mysterious ways.

There are those times when self-directed conflict management techniques do not work, when contracts, policies, and procedures are not applicable, and when someone leaving is not the desired outcome or an option. What then? In these situations, an organization may choose to hire a professional mediator to help resolve the conflict. This requires an openness and commitment to finding a resolution. It requires people being willing to embrace one or more of the conflict management techniques, in tandem with the mediator, to find an amicable resolution for all involved.

All of us who are leaders of faith are challenged to lead with integrity and faithfulness. We genuinely care about people. We give of ourselves to the organizations we serve. We work hard to accomplish the things we believe God has called us to do. Managing conflict, like it or not, is part of the equation. We will face circumstances and situations where we need to intervene. With God's help, we can choose the best approach that will result in the outcomes that benefit the organization we serve.

A LEADER'S EXAMPLE

■ A leader of a department in the organization had experienced a grievous wrong that was not only professional but also personal. One of the individuals in the department had taken it on herself to do something that violated normal protocol. To complicate the matter, she purported that the leader approved and signed off on it. The leader found out about the violation only because another organization followed up.

This incident became a major issue within the professional environment, changing the way the leader and the individual in question interacted and worked together. The leader had invested a significant amount of energy, time, and patience in helping this individual develop her professional potential. The leader trusted her, believed in her, and valued her. The leader was mentoring this individual for success. All of that changed.

The situation became very personal and ultimately adversely impacted both individuals. The subordinate felt embarrassed and humiliated. She admitted that what she did was wrong. She acknowledged that she caused the leader professional embarrassment, along with personal emotional pain, and compromised a professional and personal relationship. While the individual was remorseful, the damage had been done.

The leader was flabbergasted that this individual would do such a thing. After all the energy and time invested in helping the individual succeed, the leader felt betrayed, manipulated, and devalued. The leader was concerned about her own reputation within and without the organization. She was concerned about protecting the integrity of the department and organization. The leader was concerned about how this incident would affect future opportunities for the department.

As time passed, the subordinate knew she had to try to make things right. She wrote a letter of apology to the leader. Subsequently, she tried to meet with the leader to apologize in person. Every indication was that she was remorseful for her actions, and if not, she was at least cognizant that she needed to try to do the right thing. Likewise, she was willing to do whatever she needed to do to make things right inside the organization and, to the extent possible, outside the organization.

The leader, on the other hand, was less than amicable. She felt so betrayed and used that she refused to interact with, assist, listen to, or meet with the subordinate. If the power was all hers, she would have terminated the individual's position in the department. The leader took every step possible to excommunicate the subordinate from everything she possibly could. The leader was unwilling to take any initiative to resolve the issue. She simply drew a line between her and the subordinate and refused to do anything that would force her to cross that line. Forgiveness was not an option for this leader.

The tragedy of this scenario is that this was a faith-based organization whose leaders were to represent Christian character and conduct. One of the stated goals for all those in authority was that they were to model Christlike attitudes, demonstrate Christlike behavior, and intentionally seek to help others grow in their Christian faith. This did not mean that a person had to compromise his or her professional standards to facilitate this, but it did mean a person had to integrate Christian faith with best practices. The goal was to help people live out their faith while professionally serving others. This leader was missing the mark.

It became obvious to the leader's superiors that this leader was not living up to the organization's code of conduct. Every attempt to discuss the issue with the leader was met with resistance, an emphatic refusal to change stances, and adamant declarations of resolutions akin to excommunication. The leader simply refused to budge from her position. Unfortunately, it was turning into a human resources issue because the leader was entering the realm of insubordination and noncompliance with organizational expectations.

Perhaps what made it more tragic was the subordinate's seeing the disconnect between the stated values of the organization and what this leader was doing. This individual was not privy to what the organization was doing to address the issue with the leader. All she saw was the attitude and behavior of the leader and how she was being viewed and treated by the leader.

The Example of the Leader

The truth is, people are going to remember how a leader handles an issue more than the outcome itself. Don't get me wrong, they will remember the outcome, but they will never forget how something was handled. The subordinate above will always remember how this situation was handled. Even though she committed a grievous infraction, demonstrated remorse, and tried to apologize, the indelible imprint on her mind will be the actions and reactions of her superior.

Consequently, it is imperative that a leader conduct himself or herself in a manner that reflects the character and attitudes of what he or she professes. For leaders of faith, this should be Christ and the principles and precepts of the Word of God. If a faith leader professes to be a Christian, he or she should act like it. This requires being consistent with the walk and the talk. Every thought process, every action, every interaction, every decision, and everything about a leader's life need to reflect the firm foundation of a Christian paradigm. People are watching, listening, making mental notes, and passing judgment accordingly.

Some time back, I heard a speaker use the phrase "consistently consistent." At first it sounded redundant; however, the more I thought about it, the more I began to understand the deeper meaning. Leaders need to be consistent in their faith, their actions, their words, their reactions, and every other arena of life. In other words, there must be a likeness or harmony in everything the leader does. To do this all of the time is to be consistent. Being consistently consistent suggests the leader always acts and responds in harmony with his or her core identity and values. In some ways, it is almost predictable. People are going to look for the foundation of faith at the core of everything the leader does.

When leaders permit themselves to go unchecked and respond and react to negative stimuli in ways that are contradictory to their core values and profession of faith, they compromise everything they say they believe. People are discerning. They can see through the facade. Figuratively speaking, they can see and hear the heart. It does not take supernatural brilliance to ascertain the attitude of the heart. Faith leaders need to guard this closely, seeking the wisdom and power of God to act and react appropriately in every situation. It is a matter of being consistently consistent.

Criteria for a Leader's Actions

There may be many criteria we could elaborate on to illustrate how a leader should act and behave in managing conflict. In this section, I want to draw our attention to three key critical elements: (1) biblical foundation, (2) personal integrity, and (3) Christian spirit. While these are closely associated, each must be considered on its own merit. Each is a foundational component for a leader who finds himself or herself engaged in conflict management. Compromising on any one of these elements would be detrimental to a leader's ability to successfully manage conflicted situations and resolve issues.

Biblical Foundation

A wise leader will consult the Scriptures for wisdom and guidance when facing conflict. For centuries, preachers have declared the Bible to be a road map for life, a guidebook for living, the rule book, and more. Books have been written on doing things "by the Book." We view the Bible as the supreme written authority of God, inerrant in all things pertaining to our salvation, and as truth for daily living. If we believe all of this, and we do, then it just seems reasonable to assume that we would begin conflict management by consulting the Scriptures.

I am not suggesting that every situation and issue we face as leaders is overtly outlined and illustrated in the Scriptures.

While there are many references to attitudes, behaviors, actions, and reactions, the key to understanding a leader's ability to manage conflict is found in the principles and standards throughout the Word. Some of these are plainly detected, and others are more subtle. Whether we look at individual examples or consider the whole collectively, the one thing evident is that biblical principles are consistently consistent.

When we think about forgiveness, we think about what God has done for us and others through Christ. We are reminded about the deep sea of forgetfulness, the parable of the unforgiving servant, forgiving seventy times seven, and so much more. The principle of forgiveness is straightforward. We should forgive others as God has forgiven us. The Bible is clear on this point.

What do we do with conflict that is laced with complexity, is more difficult to understand, and may have fewer directives in the Word? Perhaps we cannot even find a scripture context or example that truly addresses the situation directly. Do we ignore a biblical foundation in favor of leaning on our own professional development and human intuition? Absolutely not! Wise leaders look for underlying principles and emerging themes to guide a framework of understanding. Throughout the Scriptures are tenets, core values, standard practices, and more, that can give a leader a contextual framework for developing a biblical conflict management approach. If the Bible is less directive, then we have to ask, What are the foundational principles in situations like the one we are facing?

Personal Integrity

A leader must be a person of integrity. Likewise, a leader must guard his or her integrity against the principalities and powers of this world. We live in a culture where integrity is purported to be valued, but the attitudes and behaviors of some leaders do not necessarily back it up. All of us can think of situations where someone compromised for a moment of pleasure, the amassing of wealth, or the avoidance of pressure. In some ways, it seems as if the dominant views of society allow us to accept situational integrity as more appropriate than being principle based and consistently consistent.

Faith leaders must rise to the occasion and always behave in ways that model Christian integrity. We said earlier that people will remember how a situation was handled more than they will remember its outcome. A sure way to lose the respect of followers is for a leader to change perspectives because of individual situations, the people involved, or the risk/consequences or in order to manipulate an outcome. If people cannot sense that the leader is principle driven, grounded in the Word of God, they will lose trust, begin to question, and ultimately lose respect. When this happens, integrity is a memory instead of a present reality.

When dealing with conflict, a leader can get pulled to one side of an issue. Likewise, it is easy to get emotionally involved and begin to see things with a biased perspective or even take sides. Leaders with integrity understand that they must remain as neutral and as objective as possible. This does not mean they do not see "wrong" as wrong and address it. But it does mean the leader takes the high road and treats all parties involved equitably and works through situations with integrity.

In some ways, one might argue that leaders with integrity are predictable. By this I mean they will always respond with Christlike manners. Previous experiences will bear this out, and their track record is true to form. The clarity of their conversation is grounded in the principles and precepts of God's

Word. The attitude of their hearts is focused on the greater good for the kingdom. Their decisions are sound. Their treatment of others is equitable. They are consistently consistent.

An agency director served a not-for-profit, faith-based ministry for a little over six years. When he announced he had accepted a new position and would be leaving the agency, there were many positive and touching comments made that expressed appreciation and value for his service and leadership. This director later reported that of all the kind things that were said, the statement that meant the most to him came from a long-tenured program director. She simply stated, "While you were here, it felt safe." Both the program director and the agency director knew what she meant; his leadership was consistently consistent.

Christian Spirit

A biblical framework of understanding and action with integrity is demonstrated in our spirit. It is the core of who we are, the way we think, the way we feel, our perceptions, the decisions we make, and the way we interact with others. Biblical integrity is expressed with a passion to honor God in all we do. It is also a deep compassion for those with whom we are doing the work of God and for those whom we are trying to reach. It really is a matter of the attitude of the heart.

As a university instructor, I often say to students, "Let me hear your heart beat." What I am asking for is openness, honesty, and genuine thoughts and feelings. Don't get me wrong, I am concerned about academics and strive to educate learners with content knowledge and best-practice application. I also embrace the challenge of helping learners see that serving Christ is a matter of the heart. Consequently, I want to know the heart of my students. I desire to help them mature in the things of the kingdom so that they may better serve God regardless of their chosen profession.

For faith leaders, it really is a matter of the heart. We can have lots of formal education or training. We can have lots of practical experience. We can be mentored by the experts. But the real value is a matter of the heart. At the end of day, the way a leader responds to people, the things a leader says, the way a leader treats others, the character a leader portrays, the love a leader demonstrates, and so much more, will speak to the maturity of his or her relationship with God. For a faith leader, a Christian spirit is critical. Without it, there is no consistency.

Preserving Relationships

Perhaps the greatest challenge in managing conflict is preserving relationships. This could be the relationship between those who are on opposite sides of an issue. It could be between those on the periphery who get drawn in or become collateral damage. It could be between those involved and the leader. It could be between those in the extended network of family, friends, and acquaintances. It could be between those at the opposite ends of a business deal. Almost always, there are people involved when we are working through conflicted situations. It is managing this dynamic that may be more challenging than finding a resolution to the issue itself.

For the faith leader, preserving these relationships is critical. Leaders do not want to offend or insult others, compromise future possibilities, or make things even more complicated. Leaders want their interpersonal interactions to be positive, affirming, and authentic. As leaders build on a biblical framework of understanding, demonstrate integrity, and exemplify a Christian spirit, managing relationships becomes a realistic goal and should produce outcomes that are pleasing.

There are some guiding principles that will help a leader as he or she sorts out conflict while trying to preserve relationships. First of all, generally speaking, the issue is not personal. By this I mean the conflict at hand is probably not about a personal attack on the leader. Typically, people are upset about a problem, a decision, a lack of progress, the way something was handled, or something else. While a leader's name may be implicated, generally the root of the feelings and expression of concern has more to do with what was done than with the leader.

Without a doubt, it is challenging to sort out the difference between the issue and the feelings accompanying the issue. People's emotions are expressed because they have a vested interest in the outcome. Likewise, the leader's emotions are active because he or she has a vested interest in the outcome and in some ways feels responsible and accountable for the outcome. It is very hard for a leader not to personalize the conflict; however, a wise leader learns to identify, discern, and control his or her emotions in the face of conflict. A wise leader recognizes that most of the conflicted situations he or she faces are not about him or her.

There may be times when the conflict is personal. For any number of reasons, the issues or attacks may be focused directly on the leader and may become very personal. When this happens, the leader needs to ascertain the heart of the issue or problem and then develop a plan using the Six Cs Model (see chap. 4, p. 54) for addressing it.

A young pastor was facing certain conflict in the church. Several unfortunate circumstances occurred that were truly out of the control of the pastor; however, people in the church blamed the pastor. "If he had done his job, this would not have happened!" It began with a couple of people who were deeply hurt by an event and allowed themselves to transform their emotions into blaming someone. The pastor was the most likely candidate. The tragedy of this was the emotional baggage that accompanied these individuals everywhere they went and influenced every decision they made. Over time, they shared it with others, and eventually their accusations were embraced by others.

This young pastor was in the midst of conflict that was very personal. Over the course of several months the pastor endured and tried to lead with integrity. Unfortunately, the pain and weight of the circumstances became more than he and his family were willing to bear, and he resigned the church. One could say he chose complacency and bowed out.

While this may have been the best option for this young pastor, it was not the only option. Many times leaders can sort through the issue, identify the problems, and find a management style to address the issue, even if it is personal. The good news is, most of the time it is not personal. A wise leader recognizes this and keeps conflict in perspective.

A second guiding principle to keep in mind is resiliency. "Resilience" is defined in part as the "ability to recover from or adjust easily to misfortune or change."[1] In the leadership environment, things are often changing and situations are occasionally met with misfortune. Leaders face and deal with diverse issues regularly. Sometimes the more responsibility a leader has, the more dynamic the environment becomes. A leader has things happening, changing, or moving all the time. Leaders are making decisions, some small and some large, constantly. In some ways, it seems as if a leader is just keeping things spinning while he or she moves from one pressing issue to the next.

This kind of dynamic tension can create intense and even stressful situations for the leader. A leader needs to be resilient. This means not only developing the mature emotional intelligence to recognize and manage the environment but also having a spiritual maturity that allows the leader to move with confidence as God guides the journey. In Proverbs we read, "Trust in the LORD with all your heart and lean not on your own understanding; in all your ways submit to him, and he will make your paths straight" (3:5-6).

A denominational district leader once advised a young pastor facing the dynamic tensions of pastoring, "Develop rhinoceros skin!" By this he meant, don't let everything get to you. Have thick enough skin so that everything does not pierce you and hurt or destroy you. Have thick enough skin that you can let things roll off your back and not weigh you down. It is kind of the complacency approach to conflict management, which in some ways allows you just to ignore or pretend the issues are not there.

A third guiding principle has to do with a leader choosing carefully those things he or she wants to engage in intervention. No doubt there are circumstances and situations that require, even mandate, that the leader engage. When these occur, the leader needs to rise to the challenge. On the other hand, there are circumstances and situations in which the leader can choose not to become involved. A leader must consider what is worth the personal investment of time and energy and balance that with the risk of getting involved.

Keeping conflict in perspective and knowing when to engage and when not to engage are critical skills for the leader.

Responding or reacting every time something happens or when conflict is brewing can be detrimental. Wise leaders choose carefully the situations and issues into which they inject themselves. Not everything is in the leader's lane.

For a leader to navigate through the issues, choosing which ones demand engagement and which ones do not, the leader must be self-controlled and disciplined. The ability to manage feelings, respond to thought processes, and control body language requires a disciplined maturity. This maturity comes from a personal walk with God, leadership experience, and knowing oneself. It is emotional intelligence infused with the Holy Spirit at work in a leader's life.

This experience of Holy Spirit-infused emotional intelligence mandates that the leader resolve any intrapersonal conflict. If the leader is struggling with personal spiritual matters, wrestling with personal conflicted situations, or personally struggling with external forces that are creating inner tension, it will be hard for the leader to be mature and objective in handling external conflict. When internal turmoil is weighing on a leader, it clouds perceptions and understandings. Leaders facing external conflicts must make sure they have resolved the internal issues first.

MAINTAINING UNITY

■ There was a second-career pastor who had started a church in a community where it was desperately needed. He served the church faithfully for several years, building a solid reputation in the community and establishing close relationships with those in the church. In many ways, this was home and the flock was family. As a matter of fact, the pastor and people became so close that they treated each other as family members might treat each other, with lots of joking and ribbing but with a bond that would transcend anything that tried to divide them.

On one Sunday, April 1 to be exact, the pastor thought it would be humorous to play an April fool on the parishioners. He planned his act carefully. He crafted every word and choreographed corresponding emotion for the delivery. When he got up to preach, he announced that he had accepted a call to another church, in another state, and would be leaving in thirty days. Needless to say, there was significant emotional reaction that swept through the congregation. There were gasps, there were tears, and there were questions and confusion.

The pastor let this play out for a few minutes and then said, "April Fools'!" He assured them he was not leaving, he had not accepted another church, and he would continue to be their pastor. He went on with the sermon, but I suspect it had less impact than the prank. As the service concluded, he reminded the congregation that the evening service would be the viewing of a film they rented.

The pastor spent part of his Sunday afternoon picking up the film projector from the local library, getting it set up, and making sure the film was ready to view. As the time approached for the evening service, the pastor and his family gathered at the church. Another local pastor and his family were there. As the starting time drew near, there was no sign of the parishioners. When it was time for the service to begin, only the two pastoral families were in attendance.

The pastor elected to wait a few minutes to see if anyone would drift into the service. As he waited, he became agitated. "The people knew we were having this film tonight. I went to all this trouble to rent the film, get the projector, and set it up—for what?" His emotions and words clearly expressed his disappointment and disgust.

Approximately fifteen minutes after the service's starting time, the pastor was about to call it a night and cancel the service. He was just beginning to put things away when the doors opened and in walked a large constituency of the church people. It was obvious the pastor was pleased to see them but bothered that they had arrived so late. Once the people were in the building, they exclaimed in unison, "April Fools', Pastor." Everyone laughed, including the pastor.

Sometimes the conflict we encounter is prompted by our own attitudes and actions. What this pastor was facing on this Sunday evening was clearly a result of his efforts to prank the people that morning. The emotions, the disappointment, the disgust, and the surprise the pastor felt probably paralleled what his parishioners felt that morning. His April fool led to the emotional roller coaster he and the church people experienced that day. Seemingly, this situation ended well; however, we will never really know the residual feelings or the long-term impact of any by-product from it.

Leaders need to check, guard, and protect their attitudes and actions. The last thing any authentic leader wants to do is engage in a conflict resulting from something that he or she started. Conflict is difficult. Trying to clean up or do damage control from something the leader did or didn't do is extremely difficult. As far as possible, leaders should avoid being the catalyst or stimulus for conflict.

With that said, sometimes leaders will be at the core of the conflict because of their position or a decision that was made. Reportedly, President Harry S. Truman had a sign on his desk in the Oval Office that read, "The Buck Stops Here." The reference was to people passing the buck or deflecting responsibility.[1] President Truman recognized that he was ultimately responsible. Those of us in leadership know that sometimes the buck stops at our desk; we are ultimately responsible.

Leaders must be able to make the right decisions, at the right times, for the right reasons. David Lieberman in his book *Make Peace with Anyone* observed that people make decisions for a variety of reasons: what feels good, what makes a person look good, and what is good or right.[2] Leaders must ascertain why they are making the decision they are making. Is it to feel good or make others feel good? Is it to look favorable in the eyes of others? Or is it just to do the right thing?

Making decisions based on what is right will have multiple benefits: (1) people will see the integrity of the leader, (2) right decisions are harder to argue against, (3) right decisions will help de-escalate the issue, and (4) right decisions lead to resolution of the conflict. When a leader makes a decision to look good or to make others look good, that leader undermines his or her integrity and that of the organization. If a leader is more concerned about being favored than he or she is about doing the right thing, that leader will eventually suffer demise as a leader. Leadership is doing the right thing, at the right time, for the right reason, for all those involved.

Striving for Unity

Organizations and churches want to see unity as part of their organizational culture. In the church, we talk about the unity of the body. In organizations, we seek respect and collegiality. Our faith traditions lead us to valuing unity as a key component and the centralizing force of harmony and togetherness. Unity is highly treasured; it is something we promote and for which we strive.

Simplistically, our perception of unity includes the absence of conflict. We may think if our organization is truly working within a culture of respect and collegiality, we will not see conflict. We tend to believe if our church is truly "one," with all things in common, we will not have conflicts. Both of these sentiments are misconceptions. The fact is, as stated early in this work, conflict will occur.

Organizations and churches consist of individuals who have differing opinions, beliefs, and values, much of which are framed on the environmental influences previously discussed. There will be times when these individual opinions, beliefs, or values collide. When they do, we may have conflict, especially if the stakes are high or the convictions are deep. People in any organization will not always agree. How they disagree is the real challenge for leaders.

The truth about unity is that it does not mean uniformity. We can still have unity and provide people opportunities to express themselves. We can hear varying opinions and provide space for people to think what they like. We can be respectful of different beliefs and give people room to live by their beliefs. We can appreciate different values and understand that not everyone values the same thing. This is respect and appreciation for diversity of opinion and beliefs.

Let us reframe this from a faith perspective. As leaders teach and model faith, people will see the beliefs and values being exhibited. People will see the consistency in the leaders' talk and walk. People will see the decisions that are being made and hopefully accept them as the right decisions at the right time, even if they do not necessarily agree with them. This creates an environment where unity can thrive, even though there may not be uniformity.

If someone cannot accept the direction of leadership due to strong opinion, misplaced beliefs, or inappropriate values, then conflict may be on the horizon. If this is the case, leaders can lead in one of two directions. As a first choice, they can see this kind of situation as a negative that will bring about adverse consequences and ultimately negative outcomes. This perspective results in a negative-conflict scenario where the leader finds himself or herself choosing a conflict management technique and working through the issues hoping for the best resolution possible.

A second choice for the leader is to see these times of conflict as opportunities to work through and help shape someone's beliefs and values or redirect his or her passion and commitment. Sometimes people just need more information, more direction, or a new challenge, or they need to feel affirmed. This kind of approach is about taking the incident and turning it into a teaching moment. The goal is to help all parties involved maintain unity even in the midst of conflict.

The leader may choose an appropriate conflict management style to work through this. Communication, cooperation, or coordination may be very appropriate for helping someone reconnect to the real work at hand. Likewise, the use of collaboration can bring someone along to the point that he or she develops a fully vested interest in positive outcomes. Why? His opinions, beliefs, and values were respected and understood.

Unity does not mean that everyone agrees with everything all of the time. What it does mean is people are unified around the things that truly matter—Christian character, vision, mission, core values, and the like. Maintaining unity by managing conflict appropriately demonstrates an appreciation for diversity and the value and dignity of everyone involved.

Fostering Restoration

When a leader must engage in conflict management, he or she will find that time and energy must be expended in fostering a restoration of relationships between those involved. For people of faith, this seems as though it would be a natural process. The truth is, as strong as the individuals' opinions, beliefs, and values were that led to the conflict, so is the power of their emotions. People may be hurt, feel devalued or underappreciated, or even be resistant to positive change. Not only will the leader be trying to resolve the conflict but also he or she may need to guide a healing process to rebuild trust and restore relationships. All of this is challenging and time consuming and can be mentally, emotionally, or spiritually exhausting.

The good news is the work of reconciliation is not totally up to the leader. Speed Leas suggests that reconciliation is not totally in the hands of people. God provides reconciliation. A leader's goal is to help create environments where reconciliation can occur.[3] As leaders use the Six Cs Model (see chap. 4, p. 54) of conflict management, they are hopefully achieving two ends: (1) management, if not resolution, of the conflict and (2) establishment of conditions for reconciliation to take place.

David Kale writes, "Our goal is conflict transformation where God is allowed to work through the conflict to bring new life into the church, providing it with power and resources it did not previously have for achieving his commission."[4] The same may be said of faith-based organizations. The goal is to allow God to be made manifest through the appropriate management of conflict so the organization can best fulfill its mission.

Leaders are tasked with lots of responsibilities, part of which include managing conflict. In conflict management, there is no easy answer, no easy way out, no closing your eyes and making it go away, and there is no such thing as a magic wand. What authentic faith leaders can count on is Holy Spirit-infused emotional intelligence. When leaders couple this with learning experiences and skill development, they can enter into conflicted situations confident and competent.

May God give you wisdom and grace as you press ahead in the adventure of being a faith leader. The next time you think the thought, or hear the words, "Keep it up and we are going to conflict," remember God called you and equipped you to manage conflict in a way that serves others, protects the organization, allows you to be true to yourself, and most of all honors him.

ABOUT THE AUTHOR

■ Dr. Houston Thompson is the dean of the School of Professional Studies, administrative dean for the School of Graduate and Continuing Studies, and director of the Doctor of Education in Ethical Leadership Program at Olivet Nazarene University in Bourbonnais, Illinois. He earned a master of church management degree from Olivet, a master of social work degree from Spalding University in Louisville, Kentucky, and a doctor of education degree in leadership and professional practice from Trevecca Nazarene University in Nashville.

Dr. Thompson's other professional experiences include pastoring churches in three states, working as a school social worker, serving as the executive director of a faith-based social service agency, and serving as department chair for the Department of Social Work and Criminal Justice at Olivet. He is an ordained elder in the Church of the Nazarene, is a licensed social worker in the state of Indiana, and holds a certificate in fund-raising management from the Fund Raising School at the Center on Philanthropy at Indiana University.

NOTES

Chapter 1

1. David Street, personal communication, ca. September 1, 1999.
2. Charles Perabeau, personal communication, ca. April 20, 2008.

Chapter 3

1. George Parsons and Speed B. Leas, *Understanding Your Congregation as a System* (Bethesda, MD: The Alban Institute, 1993), 19.
2. Norman L. Shawchuck, *How to Manage Conflict in the Church*, vol. 3, *Dysfunctional Congregations* (Leith, ND: Spiritual Growth Resources, 1996).

Chapter 4

1. Norman L. Shawchuck, *How to Manage Conflict in the Church*, vol. 2, *Conflict Interventions and Resources* (Leith, ND: Spiritual Growth Resources, 1983).
2. For examples, see forgiveness, Matt. 6:14-15 and 18:21-35; judging and personal accountability, Matt. 7:1-5; a Christian who sins against another, Matt. 18:15-17; and a woman caught in adultery, John 8:1-11.
3. Mark Quanstrom, personal communication, April 4, 2008.
4. Norman L. Shawchuck and Roger Heuser, *Managing the Congregation: Building Effective Systems to Serve People* (Nashville: Abingdon Press, 1996), 249.
5. Norma Cook Everist, *Church Conflict: From Contention to Collaboration* (Nashville: Abingdon Press, 2004), 26-34.
6. Norman L. Shawchuck, *How to Manage Conflict in the Church*, vol. 1, *Understanding and Managing Conflict* (Leith, ND: Spiritual Growth Resources, 1983), 30.
7. Ibid.
8. David J. Lieberman, *Make Peace with Anyone* (New York: St. Martin's Press, 2002), 64.

9. Shawchuck, *How to Manage Conflict in the Church*, vol. 1, *Understanding and Managing Conflict*. Shawchuck proposes five styles of conflict management: avoiding, accommodating, competing, compromising, and collaborating. He presents a matrix in which the concern for relationships and the concern for goals and interests of those involved are considered with each style.

Speed B. Leas, *Discover Your Conflict Management Style* (Bethesda, MD: Alban Institute, 1993). Leas offers six strategies or conflict management styles: persuasion, compel or force, avoid or accommodate, collaboration, bargain or negotiation, and support. Leas also provides information on knowing when and how to use the conflict management styles, as well as the probable outcomes.

Chapter 5

1. H. Stanton Tuttle, personal communication, ca. 2012.

2. *Merriam-Webster Online*, s.v. "cop out," accessed July 29, 2013, http://www.merriam-webster.com/dictionary/cop%20out.

3. *Merriam-Webster Online*, s.v. "cop-out," accessed February 24, 2014, http://www.merriam-webster.com/dictionary/cop+out?show=1&t=1393271232.

Chapter 6

1. *Merriam-Webster Online*, s.v. "confrontation," accessed July 25, 2013, http://www.merriam-webster.com/dictionary/confrontation.

Chapter 7

1. *Merriam-Webster Online*, s.v. "mediation," accessed July 24, 2013, http://www.merriam-webster.com/dictionary/mediation.

Chapter 9

1. *Merriam-Webster Online*, s.v. "vested interest," accessed July 22, 2013, http://www.merriam-webster.com/dictionary/vested%20interest.

Chapter 10

1. Stephen R. Covey, *The 7 Habits of Highly Effective People* (New York: Free Press, 1989), 205.

2. "Active Listening," *Mind Tools*, accessed July 22, 2013, www.mindtools.com/CommSkll/ActiveListening.htm.

3. Covey, *7 Habits of Highly Effective People*, 236.

Chapter 13

1. *Merriam-Webster Online*, "resilience," accessed September 24, 2013, http://www.merriam-webster.com/dictionary/resilience.

Chapter 14

1. "'The Buck Stops Here' Desk Sign," *Harry S. Truman Library and Museum*, accessed September 28, 2013, http://www.trumanlibrary.org /buckstop.htm.

2. Lieberman, *Make Peace with Anyone*, 5.

3. Speed B. Leas, *Moving Your Church through Conflict* (Herndon, VA: Alban Institute, 1996), 9-12, http://www.alban.org/bookdetails.aspx ?id=3544.

4. David W. Kale, *Managing Conflict in the Church* (Kansas City: Beacon Hill Press of Kansas City, 2003), 20.